TIM BRANNIGAN was born in Bel [barcode: D0254973] year of his life in St Joseph's Bab by his birth mother. He studied politics at Liverpool Polytechnic and returned to Belfast in 1990 where he began training for a career in the media. He went on to become an award-winning journalist, working as a reporter for GMTV's Northern Ireland bureau and then as features writer for the *Irish News* until 2003. He lives in Belfast and works as a freelance journalist and commentator, and speaks to schools, colleges and organisations about race, diversity and his life experiences.

WHERE ARE YOU REALLY FROM?

TIM BRANNIGAN

BLACKSTAFF
PRESS
BELFAST

First published in 2010 by
Blackstaff Press
4c Heron Wharf, Sydenham Business Park
Belfast BT3 9LE
with the assistance of the Arts Council of Northern Ireland

arts
council
of Northern Ireland

Typeset by CJWT Solutions, St Helens, Merseyside
Printed in England by Cromwell Press Group

A CIP catalogue record for this book
is available from the British Library

ISBN 978-0-85640-853-3

www.blackstaffpress.com

To Peggy, my beautiful and extraordinary mum. You are never far from my thoughts. Love as always.

Also for my brothers Ciaran, Paul, Damien and Declan (aka Paddy, to whom I owe a special debt of thanks for being my 'go-to guy' during the prison years). And to Chris. Thanks to you all for your support.

To my new-found brothers and sisters: this is the hand I was dealt. I will always be ready to talk.

CONTENTS

A Death in the Family

I was born on Tuesday 10 May 1966. I died the same day. Relatives hugged and cried as Mum's brothers exchanged handshakes and grimaced. My aunts wept, the men stepped outside for smokes, candles were lit and prayers were offered up to save my soul from an eternity in purgatory. The congratulatory bouquets by the hospital bed came to represent wreaths and Peggy Brannigan went from being proud mum to grieving mother.

My mother had managed to create not so much a phantom pregnancy, but rather a phantom death. As relatives prayed, I was concealed a few rooms away, blissfully unaware of everything. Mum was weaving a solemn, tearful lie to her parents, brothers, her only sister and even her three other children. Motivated by a mother's love, her plan was to pretend that she had had a stillborn baby. She had secretly confided in the staff at Templemore Hospital, including one senior doctor, about what she planned to do and though it meant risking their careers and the hospital's reputation, they had agreed to help her. Mum's husband Tom played along with the charade, mainly because she had told him a separate harrowing lie – that she had been raped.

I was kept hidden for the five days that Mum was in hospital. The brief moments of bonding between mother and child took place without well-wishers at the bedside, without greeting cards or the usual cosy clutter of celebration. There was no procession of proud relatives talking excitedly about who I looked like. The brand-new cotton babygrows, bibs, and booties were never presented; the toys were quietly put away. It was like it all never happened. It was like I never happened.

Mum had made it clear to the medical staff that while she had no choice but to pretend that the baby had died, she did at least have a clear strategy to get through the crisis. She just needed time; time to think about her next move and time to think about what she could tell her devout, Irish Catholic parents.

She was on her guard at all times. One tiny slip and the whole plan would be uncovered. When her younger sister, Kathleen, and Kathleen's husband, Al, came to visit her at the hospital, they expressed surprise that Mum was in Templemore Hospital, in east Belfast. Why wasn't she in their local Royal Maternity Hospital in the west of the city? They were taken aback when she told them that the maternity wards in the other hospitals were full. They were taken in, too, by Mum's claim that Templemore had better food than anywhere else. Kathleen knew Mum was an exceptionally fussy eater, so it made some sort of sense and besides, they didn't want to add further stress so they didn't ask too many questions.

Mum could scarcely disguise her inner turmoil. The tension spilled over. During one visit, she asked angrily why her young sons Ciaran, Paul and Damien were on the ward. Kathleen said that she just wanted them to know their mother was alive and well so they wouldn't be anxious. Mum visibly relaxed and she seemed glad to see them well turned out in their Sunday best and wearing the hats she had knitted for them.

After the visiting relatives had gone home, Mum put her plan into action. Her first task was to give her child a name, but the doctors and nurses were shocked when she told them what she wanted to call me. They told her it would be cruel to call me by the special name she had chosen. Think about the impact it would have on him as he grew up, the doctors warned. It could make his life even harder, they added. But Mum was adamant that her baby would have the particular, unusual, name she had picked.

Mum had intended to call me Ekue, a Ghanaian name pronounced Eck-way. She wanted to give me an African name because I was her black baby, fathered by a man who was not her husband. Ekue was his surname: Michael Ekue. He was a polite, suave, young doctor living and working in Belfast, whom Mum had met at a dance the previous year and who had, for a time, become the centre of her world. From the start she wanted me to be aware of my heritage and also of my father's identity. In the midst of her own troubles, she had the foresight to start leaving clues, some obvious, some less so, so that I could trace him more easily in the future. She did not expect this man to be around for the long haul, it seemed.

After a few days she finally decided to compromise. She called me Timothy and gave me Ekue as my middle name. And then, heartbroken, she handed me into the care of hospital staff. Their task was to take me, clandestinely, to St Joseph's Baby Home, also in the east of the city. In handing me over to the orphanage, she gave them one vital instruction: this baby was 'not for adoption'.

Mum's energy was drained by the stress and the thought that her long days and sleepless nights of planning might be undone by a curious relative asking an innocent but awkward question, or by a member of the medical staff letting something slip. She had already had the fright of her life when, having chosen an out-of-the-way hospital for the birth, she discovered that a woman from near her home in west Belfast was working there. This nurse realised quickly that an elaborate lie was afoot and Mum felt compelled to confess her story, appealing to the nurse's decency and compassion for total discretion.

The first searing pangs of pain and perhaps guilt came on Sunday, when Mum was preparing to leave the hospital to go home. Close to breaking point, mentally and emotionally, she was reduced to a tearful, wailing wreck by an awful coincidence. As family members arrived at the hospital entrance to take her home, I was carried to a waiting car only feet away, by a nurse who was taking me to St Joseph's Baby Home. When Mum saw me in the arms of the nurse, she became hysterical. She remained inconsolable all the way home, weeping very real tears for a very real pain. Those around her assumed she was crying for the baby she had just lost. And, in a way, they were right.

Convincing the world that I was dead was the first part of Mum's strategy. Hiding me among the abandoned infants and orphans of St Joseph's Baby Home bought her time and much-needed breathing space. Then, in the early summer of 1966, Mum began to focus on rescuing me from the orphanage and bringing me home to be with her without raising any suspicions.

The Girl in the Photograph

Peggy Brennan was born on 15 January 1933 into a working-class family in Carrick Hill, a small nationalist area at the bottom of the loyalist Shankill Road on the edge of the city centre. She was the first girl after a run of five boys. There were to be eight children in total. Her parents, Kitty and Mickey, owned the local shop and the chip shop. It was a poor area but the Brennans had a little money and a lot of respect.

Granny Brennan worked hard and was committed to helping others. Their small businesses provided them with enough income to afford a certain amount of comfort, relatively speaking. Pride of place went to a large, American gas cooker, all bells and whistles, which was far superior to anything people in the street had seen before. It had several rings and it virtually became a community resource. Granny used to cook about twenty turkeys and chickens for the neighbours in the run-up to Christmas, charging only a tiny sum for the gas. 'Kitty Brennan fed half of Carrick Hill,' said one neighbour years later.

Mickey Brennan fought in the First World War as a Lewis gunner. He joined the 6th Battalion Connaught Rangers and was posted to Ypres in Belgium, serving almost five years in its hell of blood and mud. He never spoke about his experiences but every day of his life he called into St Patrick's, St Malachy's and St Kevin's churches 'for a wee visit' on his walk around the area. Some of his devotion no doubt came as a result of the horrors he witnessed, although his own family had always had a deep sense of faith. What little the family did manage to extract from Granda about his war experiences paints an intriguing picture. He witnessed his closest friend being shot dead and also refused to follow an order to bayonet German soldiers if they were trying to surrender. In 1916, he was transferred to a hospital in Dublin suffering frostbite in his feet and lost some toes. But his sick bed was not as safe as he had hoped as republicans began their historic Easter Rising and marched into the hospital declaring Granda and other service men 'under arrest' as British soldiers. Granda took this news in good humour and, being injured, simply lay on in bed. The rising was over in a week and, eventually, Granda was sent back to the war in Europe where he was promoted to Lance Corporal in the field. His regiment was decimated on 24 March 1918 in Belgium. Seventeen of the eighteen officers were killed and of the 630 men in the regiment, only thirty survived, most of them headquarters staff that had not been active on the frontline. This makes Granda's survival even more remarkable. He was decorated for gallantry but British records show that he sent his medals back after the war. During his time in the British Army, Granda also became a boxing champion, winning a bout between British and Irish regiments by knocking out his opponent in the first round. He later became a professional boxing referee and played football too, winning gold medals for victories with Belfast team, Alton United, in all-Ireland soccer tournaments in Dublin, and representing Ireland at international level.

Granny was born in Sailortown, the docks area of Belfast. She was staunchly nationalist and would sit Mum on her knee and sing old Irish laments to her. Family lore has it that, as a young woman, Granny was arrested and fined for waving one of the first Irish tricolours ever seen in Belfast in support of the men captured during the Easter Rising. The prisoners were taken by ship to Belfast from Dublin and, as they left the docks, they were marched past Granny's house. It was then that she showed her true colours, defiantly waving her flag.

The people of Carrick Hill played host to a regiment of US soldiers during the Second World War when they were based in a derelict factory called Marsh's Buildings, only yards from the Brennan house. These soldiers were part of an exclusively black regiment and caused something of a stir in a community where many people had never seen 'coloureds' before. Mum, who was aged about twelve at the time, was fascinated by them. The black soldiers used to throw chocolate bars to children and were delighted when locals watched their baseball games and adopted US slang. With their strength and robust health, the Americans impressed the locals, who were scraping by on war rations. The military uniforms added a touch of the heroic, and with accents that evoked Hollywood glamour, the soldiers seemed like supermen to the people of Carrick Hill. Mum always had a keen interest in other people and places. She had a hope that her life would take her out of poverty and give her the chance to see something of the world. Seeing Americans at the top of her street when she was a young girl was something that moved and inspired Mum and may have helped to shape her views on other races.

Granny indulged her first daughter, buying her stylish clothes from upmarket shops because she believed they represented better value in the long run. Mum would continue to adopt this approach throughout her life, whether she was buying a new coat or a fresh loaf. She idolised the Hollywood greats and regularly took books out of Belfast Central Library to read the 'truth' about their private lives. Stars such as Lana Turner and Betty Grable fascinated her. She knew all there was to know about the movie legends but, typically, held in contempt any celebrities who gave names or information to the anti-communist McCarthy trials in the 1950s. As far as she was concerned, Ronald Reagan was public enemy number one and, decades later, when he was American President, to Mum he was still just a 'tout'.

When she was sixteen an American sailor called Bobby became her pen pal and asked her to send him a photograph. She went into town to have her portrait taken at the prestigious Ashley's Photography Studio. The family were amazed and Mum was thrilled when, a few days later, her portrait was placed in the window of the studio. While the other windows had a host of images of bonnie babies, proud military men in their dress uniforms and married couples vying for the attention of passers-by, the central section of the bay window was comparatively stark. Mum, wearing a black dress, a pearl necklace and a knowing look, gazed away from the lens: 'I know I have your attention,' she seems to be saying, 'but you don't have mine.' It announced to the world that, at sixteen years of age, Peggy Brennan the young woman had arrived. The picture knocked people sideways, from neighbours in the street to sailors on a US Navy ship. Her naval pen pal wrote to tell her he had proudly shown the picture to his pals.

As a schoolgirl, Mum had been encouraged by her teacher to visit St Joseph's Foundling Home as a volunteer, and to take the children out for walks and day trips. Even after leaving school, and indeed for the rest of her life, she kept up this voluntary work. In 1959 the home moved to a brand-new, three-storey facility and was renamed St Joseph's Baby Home. Purpose-built it may have been, but it had the requirements of the staff and administrators in mind, rather than the needs of the children. Practical, hygienic accommodation, as opposed to emotional care and a nurturing of potential is, perhaps, the best way to describe its ethos. The home was run by the Nazareth Sisters, a holy order based in the nearby Nazareth Lodge. An alarmingly large amount of children were based there. In 1966, the year I was born, there were seventy-five children being looked after by staff. At any one time there could be up to one hundred babies under three years old resident. We children were held in large, dormitory-type rooms. The sheer maths of the situation would suggest that the care on offer was primarily practical: an endless cycle of washing, cleaning and feeding. A lucky few were eventually taken home by their mothers and others were adopted, but more still stayed and weren't chosen by anyone. Most of these babies were the children of young women who had become pregnant out of wedlock, sometimes as a result of rape and incest. Those keen to adopt were spoiled for choice and the number of children available meant that checks for parental suitability were often perfunctory. There were so many babies, in fact, that people mostly ignored children with disabilities or of mixed race.

If a child had not been adopted by the time it reached three years old it was taken to a children's home – Nazareth House for the girls and Nazareth Lodge for the boys. At the age of thirteen, girls and boys were sent to a home in the small rural village of Kircubbin. It had a farm and the children were employed to look after the animals, muck out and do other manual jobs. Such work was carried out at the expense of attending school and many suffered educationally. Expect-ations were not high. The boys became farm labourers and the girls went into service in middle-class homes. As the social services and other state agencies gradually replaced the church and took on responsibility for the welfare of children, the numbers dropped markedly. By 1976 only twenty-one babies were taken into St Joseph's and by around 1980 it stopped being a baby home entirely and became a children's home.

As a young woman, Mum was so touched by the plight of children at the home that she often brought some of them to the family house as a treat. Some of those she chose were black children. Mum treated them to fish and chips and sweets and tried to give them a break from their usual austere existence. She quickly earned a reputation for being concerned about their welfare. Local kids loved her too and would regularly come to the door to ask if Peggy was coming out to play. She often did. But it was the loneliness of the black children at the home that struck a particular chord with her. By helping out at St Joseph's she learned that black children were unlikely to be adopted and were therefore condemned to a life of harsh institutional care. Little did she know then that, many years later, such kindness would be rewarded during the darkest period in her own life.

In 1953 Mum met Tom Brannigan, the man she was to marry, at an alcohol-free dance in St Comgall's school on Belfast's Falls Road. They got on well and started courting. When he was nineteen, Tom bought a motorbike – a black and chrome Royal Enfield – and Mum was happy to be the pillion passenger. In the post-war era of austerity and rations, a man on a motorbike was always going to seem glamorous. Mum enjoyed the sense of adventure of going for a spin around the area. The girl in the photograph and the man with the motorbike: they must have seemed pretty exciting to Carrick Hill's residents.

Tom was from a small family: just himself, his mum and his brother, Pat. His father died when Tom was three years old. He can remember playing with his father in the hall of their small Kashmir Road home, beside Clonard Monastery in west Belfast, but little else. As he grew up, Tom and his pals played football in the street using a ball made from paper wrapped up in a handkerchief. He was a boy soprano at his church and his mum was very protective of him, but by the time he was fourteen he had to get a job to help put food on the table, so he trained as an apprentice bookbinder. By the time he met Mum she was keen to get married because, at twenty years old, she was at the 'right' age. And there's no doubt that she was in love with Tom. The young lovers used to go cycling together in the countryside and even bought matching bikes for these awaydays.

Tom eventually sold the motorbike to buy Mum a diamond-cluster engagement ring, which she wore until much later on in her life, even after the stones had long since fallen out. She never had much luck with the ring from the moment she got it. One Christmas, she realised with horror that it was missing from her hand. It turned up in the gravy of the neighbour's turkey, which Mum and Granny had cooked for them.

The wedding was a low-key affair. White weddings were the preserve of the wealthy but, with her parents' generous financial support, Mum was beautiful on the day. She wore an expensive burgundy dress with a boat-shaped collar, which was very stylish and of its time. To begin with, the relationship was happy and carefree, but 'that all ended the minute we got married,' Tom said later.

Initially they lived in Belfast, staying in Tom's family house. Granny Brannigan was a difficult woman, given to hostility and melodrama. She and Mum didn't see eye-to-eye. Difficulties in such relationships are common enough but Mum, while up in a bedroom, overheard Tom's mother downstairs claim that Mum was trying to poison her. It was a laughable, paranoid claim but it suggested that Granny Brannigan wasn't about to relinquish control of her son without a fight. 'She wouldn't let me fry an egg,' said Tom, acknowledging that his mum always fussed over him.

At Mum's insistence, she and Tom went to England, to look for work. They found steady jobs in Nuneaton; Tom as a book-binder, Mum in a hat factory. Aunt Sally, who was married to Mum's brother Gerry, joined them and worked alongside Mum. Tom was proud that he never missed a day's work in his life. Mum was a hard worker, too. But it takes more than hard graft to make a marriage. A solid relationship requires other qualities, including trust.

After a trip to Belfast, Mum returned to their flat in England and found the sheets ruffled on the spare mattress and various drinks glasses dotted around the room. Tom explained to her that he'd met and befriended a man from Belfast and they had been in the flat chatting. Within a day or two Mum returned to Belfast distraught – she had found a packet of condoms in his pocket and love letters from another woman in a drawer in their home. That he left letters where they might easily be found might suggest he wanted to get caught but, more real-istically, he simply didn't always think things through.

Despite the tensions that had undermined their marriage

almost from the start, their first son, Ciaran, was born in Belfast in 1956. Mum wanted her children to be born in Ireland and had travelled home for the birth, alone. Paul was born three years later. While Mum only really stayed in England for five or six months, Tom stayed for over five years, despite the birth of his two sons. He resented his wife's 'fierce temper' and independent-mindedness and sought solace in glasses of beer.

In 1963, a third son, Damien, was born and Mum's parents paid for the deposit on an expensive new home in Mica Drive in the Beechmount area, off the Falls Road. The house had three bedrooms, front and back gardens and a driveway. However, financial difficulties and three children to feed and clothe only added to the tensions between the couple.

Tom did attempt to be a good father to his three sons, and the older boys, Ciaran in particular, have memories of happy times spent with him. At a time when foreign travel was unheard of and even going to the Irish Republic was unusual, Tom brought the boys to Achill Island off the coast of County Mayo for a fantastic family outing. They climbed a hillside overlooking the Atlantic and they could see a fisherman on the hill scanning the water for the basking sharks that were just off the coast – there was a shark fishery on Achill at the time and the fishermen went out to catch sharks in traditional, hand-built boats called curraghs. The dead sharks lined up on the shore fascinated the boys and Tom took photos of Paul and Ciaran standing on a shark's back.

At home, Tom used to set out plates of biscuits as a little treat for the boys' breakfast when they got up for school. He placed them by the hearth and the boys would sit by the fire gorging themselves on these chocolate-flavoured luxuries rather than a fry or the porridge they normally had. I don't remember this but when told of it I immediately doubted a telling detail. I bet my brother, who cherished the tale, that it was Mum who got up and lit the fire before going back to bed. I checked with Tom who laughed in agreement, adding that he'd never lit the fire in his life. Ciaran, my eldest brother, was slightly disappointed when I told him that it had nothing to do with Tom. 'Don't worry,' I said, 'instead of it being a lovely story about your dad, it's a lovely story about your mum.'

It would be wrong to lay all the blame for the disintegrating marriage at Tom's door. Communication seems to have been a problem. Mum's suggestion that they go to England to look for work was to benefit the whole family and earn money for a home of their own. Tom, who may not have been used to the responsibilities that marriage brought, viewed this as 'nagging'. Perhaps the bills and the children cramped his style. He certainly revelled in his role as a pub singer in amateur show band The Jaffa Trio. It was a world away from the domesticity and responsibilities that a wife and family placed upon him. Maybe he wasn't ready for marriage, or perhaps he wasn't ready for marriage to a woman as formidable as Peggy Brennan.

Mum was, by common consent, a remarkably attractive, vivacious woman, with a youthful complexion and dark brown hair. In her early thirties, she began to emerge from a life of domesticity and frustration to find a social life of her own. Tom had been indulging his passion for singing in bars and by the mid-1960s, she was feeling aggrieved, unloved and deeply suspicious of her husband's behaviour and attitude – although a sense of grievance was something they shared.

In 1965, Mum attended a dance in central Belfast with some girlfriends where she spotted a 'very handsome and very, very black man'. He walked over to their group and asked if one of them wanted to dance. One girl took exception to being asked to dance by a 'nigger'. Mum saw only that he was a tall, handsome, charismatic man and with her characteristically strong will – as well as, presumably, some raging hormones – she seized her chance and asked him to partner her at 'Ladies' Choice'.

Mum soon discovered that the black man's name was Michael and she fell for him immediately. He was everything she wanted. 'I never thought someone like him, with his background and education and breeding would be interested in someone like me,' she told me years later. She often used the word 'breeding' when describing him. As they danced, a potent cocktail of drinks, music and desire swept her off her feet and the two began a passionate affair.

'I can't believe it, I'm pregnant,' Mum informed Michael just weeks later.

'I'm married,' he said. This was a detail he hadn't mentioned before, but why would he? And Mum was married too, so she was as guilty as him. He had three children of his own and Mum was now pregnant with her fourth.

The sensibilities of her Catholic parents, the local community and Northern Ireland's 1960s provincialism all added to her predicament. The defiant streak in her nature wanted to rebel against convention and prejudice but in the end she wasn't in a position to reject them entirely. Nor did she want to bring disgrace upon her family.

Michael's response to their situation was abrupt – he didn't want to talk about it. They continued seeing one another but when they finally discussed the pregnancy Michael suggested termination. Perhaps, as a doctor, such a procedure didn't seem so alien to him, but it was a world away from what Mum was thinking. Not only was abortion illegal in Northern Ireland, Mum, like many others, also viewed it as immoral. 'Getting rid of it' just wasn't an option and Mum knew she would be left holding the baby. A black baby. She needed to come up with a plan quickly. The fear of her husband discovering her betrayal was bad enough but this was the least of Mum's worries. She agonised over what to do. Sleepless nights and shredded nerves left her exhausted.

One afternoon while walking through the streets near her home with her eldest Ciaran, she was close to breaking point. Ciaran offered her a Love Heart sweet from the packet she had bought him. As she went to eat it, Ciaran stopped her. 'No, read it, Mum,' he said. She looked at the message written on the sweet. It said simply: 'Don't cry!'

Each day she dreamed up a story to explain away the whole mess but each preposterous story was shot through with holes. 'I thought my world was caving in,' she told me. 'I had to pretend to be happy, with the pregnancy and with my marriage, but it was hell. People never stopped asking, so even if I did think about other things for a minute, something always brought the problems crashing back. It would scare me. I didn't know what I was going to do and there was no one I could tell.'

As the weeks passed, Mum knew she was running out of time. She knew she needed to speak to Tom as quickly as possible, not only because she felt a sense of duty to him but, perhaps more crucially, because he was the only one who knew the state of their relations in the marital bed – they hadn't slept together in months. For Mum, there was just no getting away with it. And the lie, when it came, was almost biblical in scale. She told Tom that a black man had raped her. To add authenticity, she also said that she had been to see a priest in St Patrick's Chapel in Donegall Street for advice. The spiritual guidance, Mum told Tom, was that they should simply support each other and deal with the consequences. Tom agreed to do as the priest suggested. He was extremely compliant and did not suggest going to the police. Nor did he demand much in the way of details when told this shocking news. Whether he believed the story completely remains unclear. 'So, what are we going to do about it?' he asked, simply.

Mum just couldn't bring herself to confess to anyone, not her parents, or even her best friends, the truth about her pregnancy. No, she had to keep up appearances, no matter what it took. But how? As her due date drew closer, it was her work with St Joseph's Baby Home which came to mind.

White Lies

By Christmas 1966 it seemed that family life had returned to normal in the Brannigan household. I was still in St Joseph's but the upset surrounding my birth and subsequent 'death' had abated. As far as everyone was concerned, Mum was getting on with her life, working and raising her children. But she was still leading a secret life. At weekends, Mum would go to St Joseph's to visit the children, as she had always done. After a few weeks, she started bringing me home to stay in her home for a night or two. But she had done this with children a number of times before. Everything seemed normal. The journey to return her baby to the orphanage each Sunday meant tears and trauma for her, but she tried to disguise it and people pretended they hadn't noticed.

Tom, believing, or pretending to believe, that his wife had been raped, avoided asking any difficult questions. But there was still an atmosphere of point scoring between him and Mum as the damage their infidelities inflicted on the marriage became apparent. Yet Tom, whatever his issues with Mum, didn't blame me. He was delighted to have me home for visits and was happy to drive up to the baby home at weekends to collect me and leave me back. He played with me and bounced me on his knee. 'I loved you to bits,' he told me much later.

Mum, meanwhile, was still dealing with the fact that I was in St Joseph's. Given her years of volunteering at the home there must have been a deep level of trust between her and the staff and she had discussed the situation around my birth with the Mother Superior. Despite this, no one knew better than her how bad it was to be a black baby in that home. But Mum had to time my coming home to live with her and my brothers very carefully.

I was put in the home first and foremost to buy Mum time and space. She was concerned about protecting herself, her wider family and me from disgrace. She was also trying to protect her flawed marriage, for economic as much as romantic reasons. Mum knew she had fooled most people by pretending the baby had died but she was paranoid that some might harbour suspicions about a possible affair. She could never be certain that her friends – the ones who were there when Mum first met Michael – would fall for her cover story. That was the main reason why I was placed in the home. Had I been white, I'm sure Mum would have simply taken me home and acted as if nothing was wrong. Mum's problem was that I was black.

She decided that there needed to be a cooling-off period after all the drama – a drama that, until the second I was born, was only ever played out in her head since everyone else was unaware of her dilemma. Driven by stress and anxiety, she settled on what was probably an over-elaborate ploy – to wait for someone other than herself to suggest that she adopt me. Once she made this decision, she had to wait for someone – anyone – to make the suggestion. There were lots of chats, family functions and Sunday afternoon visits when people called, but no one mentioned adoption. Why would they? She had three children and could easily try again for another if she wanted, relatives might reasonably have assumed. This may account for the length of time that she allowed to pass before she brought me home from St Joseph's. And while I was in there, Mum got another shock as she watched a local TV news programme.

A feature on how various organisations would cope over the Christmas period selected St Joseph's Baby Home for a report. As the camera panned around the room to show all the orphaned babies, Mum spotted me among the throng. When the camera stopped on her baby she filled with emotions, including anger. 'Right, that's it!' she thought. 'I'm going to get him out of there as soon as I can.' She was desperately upset that her baby was portrayed as an orphan. 'He *has* a mother,' she wanted to tell the reporter.

Once she had stopped thinking emotionally, she realised that she would still need to exercise some caution. There was to be no melodramatic homecoming. I was, of course, still brought home at weekends, but this was Mum simply following the same routine she had over the previous twenty years, so far as family and friends were concerned. Happy as she was to have me with her in her own home, the heartbreak of taking me back to St Joseph's every Sunday was unbearable. Nonetheless, this ritual went on for months before, finally, someone made the comment she had been desperate to hear.

It happened to be my uncle John-Joe: 'Peggy,' he said, 'it's obvious that you are very attached to this wee boy. Why don't you adopt him as your son to make up for the child you lost?' And with that innocuous comment, after ten months or so, the plan to bring me home permanently finally fell into place. The idea of a fake adoption had been part of Mum's plan all along. Whether she needed to wait on someone else suggesting it is debatable – in the long run, most people never knew that it was her brother's suggestion. It may have helped fool her parents, though, and that was a consideration that weighed heavily on Mum's mind. She was able to claim, plausibly, that I was another of the black kids she always brought home, randomly chosen by her from those in care. 'I just told everyone I felt sorry for you in that home,' she told me years later. 'Everyone knew black children didn't get picked for adoption, so people were sympathetic and didn't think to question anything.'

While the British media would certainly have influenced attitudes in Belfast, there were differences between it and British cities. In Belfast communities the arrival of one black baby was regarded as a curiosity, something cute. In post-war

Britain, immigration had been encouraged en masse by organisations such as London Transport to fill low-status jobs, prompting a rapid transformation, racially, of British society that unnerved some white British people. They were apprehensive about the changes and viewed the immigrants with a level of suspicion and in many cases hostility and naked aggression. In Northern Ireland, I may not have been unique but I was certainly a rarity, a 'novelty' as some people described my presence. No one in Belfast felt 'swamped' by my arrival.

All of these factors: the society we lived in, a lack of cynicism among people in Belfast and some smart thinking on Mum's part came together and helped make her plan a success. But there was no great fanfare when she took me home; it was not the return of a prodigal son. She had taken me home for the weekend with every intention of bringing me back to St Joseph's, when I fell ill with the measles. I had to wait until I had recovered before the home would let me return. I was with Mum for a week or a little longer and she just picked up the routine. Everyone got used to me being around and Mum never bothered taking me back. That was it; I was home. The authorities in the home did not do any follow-up checks, suggesting that they were more than happy to have another child taken off their hands. They would obviously have known that Peggy was my mother, so there was no real legal barrier to taking me home. Mum basically used St Joseph's as a long-stay crèche for me until she figured out a safe way to ease my entry into the family home permanently.

Although Mum and Tom were still trying to keep their marriage together when I was brought to live at home – they even had another son, Declan (we knew him by his nickname, Paddy), together in October 1967 – it was clear that the relationship was in serious trouble. In the spring of 1968, Tom was minding all of us in the house and became agitated that Mum had not arrived home at the time he expected. He went to the front door to see if there was any sign of Mum and saw her getting out of a car halfway down the street. Tom asked Mum who was driving the car as she swept by him and into the living room. He got a forthright response: 'That's my boyfriend,' Tom claims she said of this mystery driver. Whether she was in bad form or was being provocative remains unclear. 'Right, that's it!' Tom said in reply. He got his coat and, without ceremony, walked out of the house for good.

Tom kept in touch with the older boys after the split and took them on runs across Northern Ireland in his McVitie's lorry, even as the Troubles were well under way. Paddy and I were too young for such adventures. Damien and Paul were with him as he returned to Belfast after one delivery run, only to find that rioting had swept across the city. There were some token attempts at hijacking the lorry on the republican Falls Road and near the loyalist Shankill Road but the boys' little faces must have been Tom's lucky charm. To this day, he is unsure why both loyalists and republicans waved his lorry – a prime target for burning as it was a commercial vehicle – through while others burned. It was typical of Tom though: mayhem to the left of him, carnage to the right and he sails on through, seemingly unscathed.

Within a year of Tom leaving, Mum was working in a bar near Queen's University when a man from Dublin began to small talk with her. His name was Chris Ryan. He asked if she wanted to go to the movies, which she did. They began dating and within a few months Chris moved into our house. But change at home was about to be overshadowed by growing political unrest and we, as a family, were about to find ourselves caught up in more dramatic events and extraordinary circumstances.

Troubles Ahead

'Right, Tim, you be on my team and you can be Eusebio,' my older brother Paul said as we kicked a ball outside our door. Eusebio was a black Portuguese superstar at the time. I didn't mind being called Pelé or Eusebio because I enjoyed playing football, but it stung if someone I didn't know said it to or about me. From an early age I was able to detect when a name, even a foreign name, was meant as a compliment and when it was an insult. Tone of voice was usually the giveaway, and context also had a lot to do with it. Soon it became easy to tell when hostile names were being directed my way. Sometimes it was blatant and I remember being called a 'fucking nigger' at the age of four. Older people used 'nigger', younger people tended to use more childish terms. 'There's a sambo!' an older boy said when I was in the playground at school. Sometimes people called me names when I walked along the street, usually when I was in another area: 'Look, there's Michael Jackson!' I'd look around to see someone pointing at me while other people laughed. I never reacted to these names, just dropped my head and avoided eye contact. At times people sensed my discomfort and they might either chastise the person making the comments, or at least tell them to keep it down a bit; sometimes they just laughed. 'How would you like it if you were like that?' said one schoolgirl to her friend who had just called me 'Sambo'. She was at secondary school, a teenager. I was about eight years old. I was glad of her kindness but the term 'if you were like that' has stayed with me all of my life. Some people viewed my colour as a condition, an illness or a disability.

In the 1970s, there used to be a TV show for young people featuring the adventures of a young black boy on some savannah in Africa. I can barely recall it now but the boy was called 'Yow', it rhymed with the word 'wow', although I'm guessing it was spelled differently. Some boys in my class used to shout 'Yow' when I entered the room. The teacher asked those involved what was so funny. One of them said, 'Sorry miss, I sat on a tack.' The feeling of anger and of being power-less to do much about it burned into me.

Outside of school was much worse, though. It was soldiers from the British Army who introduced me to the full range of racial insults when their foot patrols began appearing in our street. 'Oi! Look! A fucking paddy nigger! What to fuck are you doing over 'ere, then?' they shouted. Sometimes I was simply walking back from the shop with some bread and milk and from behind a car, or by a garden gate, a crouching British soldier would hiss, 'They got you bastards over 'ere an' all 'ave they?' One of my earliest memories is of a foot patrol of Scottish soldiers shouting terrible, racist names at me as I stood in the back garden of my home. I was about six years old at the time. A woman soldier with blonde hair shouted at them to stop it. She made an apologetic gesture to me as her patrol headed on its way.

But the Falls Road was hardly some enlightened oasis of ethnic togetherness where only the British Army meted out the racism. The people of Belfast were no different than people from anywhere else. They watched the same television shows and characters as people in Britain (Alf Garnett, *The Comedians* and *Love Thy Neighbour*) and they watched politicians such as Enoch Powell raise the temperature of political debate with ominous warnings that immigrants were going to lead to the destruction of British society. People in Belfast read sensation-alist reporting from the tabloid press and were influenced by it.

This meant that they were just as conversant with racist terminology like 'coons' and 'niggers' as the people of Birmingham or London, despite the fact that there were no black people to speak of in Belfast.

The only place where racist remarks were never made to me was in my own street and in a few surrounding streets. The children I grew up with saw me as just another kid who lived beside them. I was useful at football, I wasn't likely to lead anyone into trouble and I mixed well. I was just Tim. I learned very quickly that if I saw two or more people who didn't know me or only had a vague awareness of me then there was a good chance that they would first joke among themselves and then shout across at me. If I was very unlucky they would come up to me, although such attentions rarely got physical. However, one guy my age seemed to delight in threatening violence against me. He would pretend to throw punches and once he grabbed me and held me against a wall. One grey Saturday morning, I was pushing my bike across waste ground when he appeared on his bike. My bike had little red reflectors sticking out from each side on aluminium arms. This boy circled me on his bike trying to get close enough to kick the frame, the reflectors or me. I was full of nervous tension. My own street and safety were just yards away but no one could see this bully. When I tried to head in the direction of my street he would speed up to cut me off and he could see that I was nervous. 'Nigger' was the only word he said to me in a staccato, hate-filled voice, usually as he swung a boot at me or my bike. People watching from a distance could not see much wrong in his behaviour. He wasn't always so restrained in his language. His favourite chant, sung in an affected southern American accent, was: 'Bless my heart, bless my soul, I've never seen a nigger with a wee white hole!'

However, such attentions were most definitely only occasional. Usually it was limited to the odd remark when I was passing. I believe there was a good reason for this reluctance on the part of people to abuse me: the IRA. It's not that they became my personal bodyguards, but rather that their actions against the British crystalised people's opinions about the key issues of the day. The armed struggle tapped into the main faultline in Irish politics – our attitude to the British and our desire for basic civil rights at the very least and ideally, self-determination. I didn't experience as much racism as I might have because many people had a benign view of black people, partly motivated by the old maxim: 'my enemy's enemy is my friend'.

When I was a child, the debate about race had been inflamed by Enoch Powell's provocative 'Rivers of Blood' speech and the attendant rise in racist sentiment in England. Irish people knew that the signs put up by landlords in London proclaiming that they did not want black tenants also told the world that the Irish were barred too: 'No Blacks, No Dogs, No Irish'. And it was Karl Marx, I believe, who compared the relationship between English and Irish workers to that of 'the poor whites to the niggers in the former slave states of the USA', not because of colour but because 'nigger' came to refer to the poor and disenfranchised of any nation.

When the Civil Rights movement started in Northern Ireland in the late 1960s, it was inspired by the American Civil Rights Movement and by the dignity of Martin Luther King. Irish nationalists even adopted the song 'We Shall Overcome' as their anthem. The Irish saw Britain as the old enemy. Our relationship with Britain informed our sense of being the underdog. Irish people have a willingness to forge alliances with other oppressed peoples in South Africa or Palestine. Often this solidarity was little more than a state of mind but it tipped the scales just enough that to be racist was to have crossed a line. It would be wrong of me to over-state this, but in general terms, these factors and a basic common sense of decency among my community certainly helped me.

*

In January 1972, in Derry, the paratroop regiment shot dead thirteen people with many more injured. One of the injured died several months later of his wounds. I do not recall Bloody Sunday itself and I don't remember watching the news. I do, however, remember walking down the street in the rain just after it. Black flags flew out of the windows of many houses and I knew that it was because 'the Paras' had killed Catholics. Two days later, in the afternoon, there was a bit of commotion at our house and some men came into our kitchen. One of them anxiously peered out the window to make sure the coast was clear. Our back garden had a white wooden fence around it and beyond that was the brickworks. The men were annoyed because girls from St Rose's Secondary School went past our house as a shortcut to get to the Ballymurphy area. Our back door was wide open. One of the men urged the others to hurry up. Eventually they produced a 303 rifle and another guy, lying on his belly on our floor, began to test fire it. He aimed at the fence, pulled the trigger and a shot rang out. The recoil of this large rifle was so strong that it caught him off-guard and the rifle jumped up, hitting him in the face and busting his lip. They fired two or three shots, I think. I stood at the kitchen sink. The sound of the gunfire shocked me – it was different in terms of sound and volume from the gunshots I had heard on TV shows and westerns. The men asked me and my friend from across the street to go into our garden and arrange some bricks that were sitting in our garden and were going to be used to build a proper garden wall. We stacked the bricks for target practice for the IRA as they prepared to hit back against the British. They wanted to fire another round but weren't sure if there was anyone watching. I stepped forward and, acting as lookout, went to the doorstep and looked over to the school path on my right. Some girls in navy blue St Rose's uniforms were looking back at me slightly anxiously. They weren't sure what was going on and walked with hesitating footsteps up the path, peering over to our door all the while. They laughed and screamed as they headed up towards the hills. What I was witnessing was the IRA preparing to give their response to Bloody Sunday. On television John Hume was telling the world that it was a 'United Ireland or nothing' for nationalists. His words echoed in nationalist homes across Northern Ireland – homes like ours. The bloody conflict was intensifying and my family was right in the thick of it. I was six years old.

Kola Kubes and Gelignite

B y the early seventies Mum was on tablets for her nerves and there seemed to be a national epidemic of people on Valium. She was so stretched, so stressed and so tired trying to keep the family together and a roof over our heads that she even forgot to enrol me at primary school when I was five years old.

When I started school the next year I loved it from the start. On my first day boys were crying as their mums left them at the doors. One boy in our class slapped the window and wailed as he watched his mum make her way down the winding path. We lived beside the school so I was familiar with it. On my first day I sat by the window and could see our house. I could see Mum if she was in the back garden and I often saw her running down the side of the house to work, late.

At home things were complicated and Mum's behaviour was often confusing. Sometimes, without warning, at any point in the day or, more usually, in the evening, she would ask me to stand in the pantry in our kitchen. She had one simple instruction that was directed at me in a conspiratorial whisper – a plea not a threat: 'Do not make any noise and do not come out of the pantry until I tell you. Now, do not come out.' She would close the door over but a faulty lock meant it always stayed open a crack. Sometimes I was there an hour and, on some occasions, a good bit longer. There were two things I knew for certain. Firstly, it only happened when people called to the house unexpectedly. They also seemed to be people I didn't know very well. And second, complete silence on my part ensured that Mum would be happy with me. Not once did visitors detect my presence.

Years went by before I learned what it was all about, when Mum pointed out something I had never considered. It was simply that friends from her old stomping ground, Carrick Hill, would call to visit, which would have been fine except that some of them used to socialise with her on nights out and were aware that she had a bit of a thing going with Michael. They certainly saw her dance with him in 1965. Mum was worried that they would do the maths in terms of my age and realise that I was actually her son. It was as simple as that.

Over the years she grew to hate people calling to our home unexpectedly. This was, in part, down to the nervous and stressful associations she made between a knock at the door and her having to hide her secret. I was, perhaps, a constant reminder to her of the biggest scandal in her life, although she never, ever said this. For my part, I didn't even know there was a secret or that I was it. This made it difficult to play Mum's game. I have never felt that she was being cruel. She was just maintaining the fiction she had created to protect me – and herself.

One particularly nosey woman did see me in the house. I had been out when she called and I simply walked in the back door when Mum and her were chatting. I recognised immediately that Mum was extremely edgy and noticed she kept trying to cut across the conversation by sending me to get a drink of lemonade and other such diversionary tactics. I could feel the tension.

'Oh! Who's this wee boy?' said the woman.

'That's our Timothy,' said Mum, giving away as little as possible.

'Is he yours, Peggy?'

'Ach, yes. Have you not seen him before?'

'And how old are you, Timothy?'

'Are you not going out to play, love?' Mum interjected, before I could answer.

'What class are you in, Timothy?'

'He's very shy,' said Mum. 'He likes to go out and play. Go out to your friends, love.'

The woman was trying to work out what age I was to see if it synchronised with the time Mum was meeting Michael. Mum was frantic; worried that she was about to be uncovered. Given that she had kept her secret hidden from everyone, she was obsessed with trying to keep on top of every single risk to her story.

Throughout the 1970s, until about 1978, I was used to men and women calling to our house and leaving again with little ceremony. Sometimes they arrived, mumbled a few words but seemed quite agitated, or they whispered in the raised voice sort of way that people do when arguing in public. Occasionally, there was something comical about it all. It was certainly exciting for a young boy. One Saturday afternoon a man in a black leather jacket called to the door and asked a favour of Mum. She was about to fall for the oldest trick in the book. The man, a republican, asked her if they could use our back bedroom for a 'meeting'. She agreed and then sat in the kitchen nervously wondering aloud what they would be meeting about. She warned me to stay out of the room but I pretended that I needed to go the toilet.

I walked up the stairs only to hear a man whose voice I didn't recognise giving a lecture on pistols to about six IRA men in our back bedroom. 'This,' he said dramatically, with a pause for further effect, 'is a Walther PPK.' His voice was deep and he seemed very serious. I immediately tiptoed back downstairs. It was a few days later, while playing around with my brother, that we discovered a small amount of IRA weapons under the bed, including pistols and rifles, some of which seemed about one hundred years old; like something from the First World War. Mum confronted someone on our doorstep. 'I want that stuff out of here now!' she said in a hushed shout to a man who said he'd be back soon. And that was the trick Mum had fallen for. The IRA tells you they need a room 'just for a wee meeting' but when they leave you discover that they have left a little present of guns and or explosives. Sometimes, as was the case with Mum, they took advantage of people's good nature but usually people knew when stuff had been left. Mum's attitude to all of this was far from simplistic. It was a complex situation parentally, politically and morally. People were being killed, the British Army were hostile, the unionists intransigent and the IRA was, whether people like this fact or not, the only organisation we could see doing anything about it.

And they would do something about the Brits at any time of the day or night. My brother Paul opened the door one morning to find two IRA men on the doorstep. They asked for Mum and Paul told them that she was in bed. The men wanted to collect an M1 Carbine and a Lee-Enfield 303. The weapons were under the bed but not on the bedroom floor. They were actually under Mum's mattress and the men decided that national liberation couldn't wait on Mum getting out of bed so they raced upstairs, apologised, lifted up her mattress, reached under and retrieved the rifles as she lay in the bed. Mum just went back to sleep.

It all got a bit crazy. One event I didn't witness, and wish I had, was when a man I know used a parked lorry full of beer kegs at a Falls Road bar as cover for a sniper attack on British soldiers standing a few hundred yards down Broadway. The soldiers fired a fusillade of shots back. They didn't hit the sniper but rounds struck the beer kegs sending jets of foaming beer in all directions. Sometimes growing up in Belfast was like living in the wild west.

Collecting souvenirs of the conflict became a pastime for nationalists, especially young people. A little parachute attached to a canister was not an Action Man toy, I soon discovered. It was, in fact, a spent flare which was one of many fired into the air by the British Army to light up the fields and playing pitches at St Paul's Secondary School which was situated not far from our back door. The army had taken over the school as a makeshift barracks. We also had rubber bullets and, later, plastic bullets that could be found strewn in streets and lying in the gardens of Belfast's terraced streets, a testimony to the amount and ferocity of the rioting in our areas.

Sometimes when Mum was at work in one of her succession of casual jobs, republicans used our house. I once went into a bedroom and looked under the bed. The IRA rifles were back again. They were mostly wooden with some metal bits. They looked old and some of them resembled guns I saw in a book we had at home, *The British Army in Ulster* by David Barzilay. There were three or four volumes; I think we had two of them. They were notable mainly for photographs of bomb scenes, weapons finds and British Army foot patrols in hostile areas during ferocious riots. When older, I realised these books were not objective journalistic examinations of the war in the north but were in fact shameless, glossy PR for the British Army. Still, the pictures and detailed captions made for a rough guide to weaponry; Lee-Enfields, 303s, M1 Carbines and M15s were all illustrated in a way that made them seem like objects of desire; exciting and alluring. To not only see but actually hold and play with them in our house was thrilling beyond belief.

Many of my memories are of events that took place on Saturdays. One weekend a man called and asked us to clean bullets and arrange them by size and calibre. I didn't know what calibre meant so I just put the ones that looked the same into the same piles. The men left two plastic shopping bags of gelignite behind our sofa. I wondered why it wasn't called dynamite like it was on TV, as it looked the same. Individual cylindrical sticks of a gel-based explosive – hence the name – were wrapped in greasy brown paper. I wanted them to be red like in the cartoons. I was told to say nothing to anybody about this and was proud that I never mentioned it in school.

I remember one day some men came to our house and installed themselves in our kitchen. I was told to stay in the living room. Amid mumbles, whispers and occasional excitable exchanges, a man shouted in to me, 'Here, kid, have youse any fuse wire lyin' about?'

'I don't know. I don't think so.' I said, wishing I could be more helpful.

'Do youse have any Brillo Pads?'

'Yeah, I'll get them.'

I wanted to see what they were doing so I walked into the kitchen and over to the cupboard under the sink, producing a box of Brillo scouring pads. I had a quick glance and could see electrical wire, tape, pliers and a bedroom alarm clock strewn across the kitchen floor. The clock's glass face had been removed and the minute hand had been deliberately bent at a right angle so that its tip pointed up to the ceiling as the clock lay on its back on the floor. A man slowly and deliberately applied a strip of electrical tape to the top edge of the clock and pulled it across the clock face from the number twelve down to the six. I could see that if the minute hand was wound up it would eventually come into contact with and slowly cut through the tape. I had a good idea what this meant; this was a time bomb. It wasn't that difficult to work out, to be honest, because *Road Runner*, *Tom and Jerry* and any number of TV cartoons featured similar devices.

One of the men asked me if I would pull thin strands of metallic wire off the Brillo pad and twist them together to make a sort of metallic piece of string. I did this for a few minutes before being told to go back into the living room.

A close escape happened during a torrential rainstorm. A couple of my brothers and I were sitting in the living room when there was a knock at the door. My heart sank when I heard unmistakable English accents and several members of the British Army came into the house. A search! 'We're here to look for members of PIRA,' the soldier in charge claimed. By 'PIRA' they meant the Provisional Irish Republican Army. (It was a very British thing to use the terms 'PIRA' or 'Provos'. We said 'the boys' or in later years almost always 'the Ra'.) Their search was not to be as rigorous as most. It was raining hard, the type of rain that speared through the black air, illuminated only by the orange glow of the streetlights before it smashed into the street and splashed up again an inch or so into the air. The soldiers were, to a man, drenched, and we soon realised that they were delighted to get out of the deluge. They all seemed to jockey for position in front of our open coal fire and I watched as a soldier stood in front of the flames, steam billowing off his wet army trousers. They were more polite than normal and the questioning seemed hesitant as if they were going through the motions.

My reaction was a mix of hoping they'd leave and curiosity about what would happen next. Fortunately for us, the British Army foot patrol was equally casual in their attitude to their searching. I don't even think they went upstairs. If they did so, it was probably a token effort. We all breathed a heavy sigh of relief and laughed at our good fortune as, undiscovered by the Brits, a dozen brand-new rifles were stashed in a fairly devil-may-care way behind our sofa.

Real searches, when they came, were disruptive but for a young boy they could be thrilling. The first sound we heard, if we heard it, was the whiney roar of army Saracens. We called the vehicles 'pigs'. Heavily armoured, with massive wheels like the rear wheels of a JCB tractor, they were like light tanks for urban use. Some had six wheels and we called them, none too imaginatively, 'sixers'. If the sound of the pigs roaring up the street didn't alert us, the thunderous knock on the door usually did the trick.

'Jesus, Mary and Joseph – it's the Brits,' Mum would say. The normal procedure involved all of us being brought into our living room and told to sit down. An RUC officer and a British Army Commanding Officer formally introduced themselves to us. These two would then order all soldiers involved in the actual search to be frisked down. Their bulky army flak jackets, belts, flasks, guns, medical packs and other pieces of kit were left outside. The point was that this would reassure us that they were not about to 'plant' any weapons on our property; we felt no such reassurance. They would then head into all rooms of the house including the attic and begin to search. Mum was often embarrassed if the house was untidy. Our cupboards were stuffed with broken toys, old clothes, badly scratched Suzi Quatro records and general bric-a-brac. They usually arrived at 4 a.m. and it would take a few hours. I found it all very exciting especially if there were no weapons in the house. It was as if we were getting one over on the British Army.

Some of our little victories were close-run things. My older brother Paul came running into the living room late one afternoon, 'There's Brits everywhere! They're digging up gardens and everything.' I went to the front gate and could see soldiers with metal prods piercing the soil of two gardens of our neighbours. Both homes belonged to families with strong republican connections. We feared we'd be next. 'Timothy, Damien, empty your schoolbags.' I took my books out of a beige canvas bag with brown, imitation leather piping. 'Close the door! Close the friggin' door!' said Paul. I realised something was in the house. Paul began to fill my bag with explosives. I didn't really get to see what they were but there was a lot of glass. He handed me my schoolbag. 'Be careful, now. Don't say a word. Just walk past the Brits down to Finn's house and tell them we're about to get raided. They'll know what to do. Not a word, Tim. Do you hear me?'

It was early evening on a winter's day. I was hoping we wouldn't get caught because I wanted to get my tea. People stood in the street watching the commotion and army vehicles were parked at the bottom of the road. British soldiers were everywhere. I walked gingerly, scared that whatever was in my bag – which was now strapped to my back in the way primary school children wore their bags – might smash and blow us all up. The Brits thought nothing of the little black kid and his brother walking down the street with their schoolbags. I remember laughing when we walked back up our street a couple of minutes later to see the Brits digging in gardens. We went into the house and waited on them calling but they never did.

I never befriended the black soldiers in my street. I knew this was a step too far and it became easier to blank them out. They might be crouching behind a car or in a doorway to avoid sniper fire. When I passed they sometimes gave a cheery 'Hello' or asked 'What's your name, then?' As I got older I realised that I wouldn't be shot dead or tarred and feathered if I engaged them. It was really just a question of judgement and the atmosphere at the time. The black soldiers were never hostile to me. Never. Sometimes I said 'Hello' or 'All right?' as I passed them but mostly I just gave a nod or a smile of acknowledgement.

When I was about eight or nine years old a black soldier taking cover in the pathway of my friend's house called me over. He handed me a pound note, which seemed like a lot of money to me. 'Take it,' he said, handing over the green note. I shook my head silently. He smiled a broad smile exposing what seemed to me to be extremely pinkish-red gums and ivory white teeth. His skin was much blacker than my own and this fascinated me. 'Go on, take it,' he repeated in a strange accent. I reached over and took the money. 'Do you know where the IRA are, then?' Without comment, I handed him back the money and went over and stood by my own gate.

It is worth pointing out at this stage that for all of their faults – and I am not blind to their faults – the IRA did not abuse me in the systematic way that the British Army did over the first few decades of my life. Individual republicans may have done so and often I challenged them, or others challenged them on my behalf, but compared to the naked aggression and racism of the RUC and the British Army they were no problem at all. The foot patrols were heavily armed groups of eight, sixteen or even twenty-four soldiers. I had to run the gauntlet at times.

Even my Belfast accent singled me out as a target for the Brits. Often they would ask me to state my name or simply just order me to 'say something' to confirm that I had an Irish accent. If I spoke, my accent became a target for mockery for the Brits and a considerable humiliation for me, as soldiers crowded around to hear for themselves.

My whole childhood was a learning process for me; a negotiation about when and how I could be myself and times when I needed to keep my head down, stay quiet or simply get away from a situation altogether. In spite of my general acceptance within my own community, there was one incident that made me shockingly aware of my own difference.

While at primary school, Mum bought me a very colourful headdress of the sort that Sitting Bull or other Native American chiefs might have worn. The feathers were vibrant yellow with red, black and white tips. When I put it on my head it hung right down my back. I loved it and wore it proudly one afternoon as I stood at my front door. I was sure the older boys getting out of school would be jealous of this fantastic present. As part of the look, I also had a little rubber tomahawk. My pride in owning this fabulous toy, though, disappeared in a heartbeat as the boys getting out of school saw me and started shouting, pointing and laughing. They made war-cry noises of the type 'Indians' in John Wayne movies did. They called me 'Sambo', 'Geronimo' and other names. Even though I was at my own front door, I felt vulnerable and ashamed. Why did I think people would be jealous? Why did I not see this was only going to provoke such comments? I wanted to take the headdress off but was stiff with fear. I was full of silent rage. This shouting seemed to reach a crescendo then ease off as some of the boys walked on down the street. I went back into the house and didn't wear the headdress again. While the outfit disappeared, I soon learned that feeling isolated, picked on and, as a consequence, angry was to become a regular fact of life as a young boy. Mum would always tell me that there were bad people who would say things to me and that I should ignore them and feel pity towards them. It's advice I take on board now, but back then I was just anxious about it all. I tried to keep my head down.

Old women would often say, 'Give us your curls, son' while rubbing my hair affectionately in a 'you little scamp' sort of way. Occasionally girls would say, 'You're a lovely colour, I wish I was your colour.' It was nice to hear people saying things like this as it was rare, in those days, to hear black people or black skin referred to in positive terms. Ususally when my colour was mentioned it was in negative terms. I did feel negatively about myself in this context – how could I feel otherwise? In our living room one afternoon, when I was very young, my brother Paddy said I would always be black. I asked Chris, Mum's partner, if this was true and why the palms of my hands were white. 'That's the way you are, it'll always be like that,' he said. I never asked about it again but I was a little upset that I would always be different. I hated being the odd one out. I never thought of myself as adopted, although I knew many people assumed I was. What else would a black boy be doing in a white family? I viewed the word, the very idea of my being adopted, negatively. Deep down I knew it must be the case but in my day-to-day family life I never felt special or different from my brothers – except that I was black. I felt I was at the centre of the family because I was so close to Mum, but I knew that to those outside our family I looked like an outsider.

I went back to playing street games such as 'Japs and Germans', where we pretended to be fighting the Second World War (despite the fact that the 'Japs' and Germans were on the same side), but these games were soon replaced by 'Brits and Rioters'. Some of us used bin lids as shields while others threw bricks with varying degrees of accuracy at head height and with considerable velocity. In the spoils of war we got our hands on a British soldier's helmet complete with visor. I soon learned that this only caused kids to throw stones even harder, so being a rioter was always safer. We had the odd song or chant, too. One went to the tune of 'Jesus Christ Superstar', a musical hit at the time:

> Jesus Christ Superstar
> How many Brits have you shot so far?
> Ninety-one, with a Thompson gun
> One was lucky and he got it in the bum.

We grew up in a world where the abnormal seemed normal and scenes other people found remarkable went by unnoticed for us. On trips into town, I joined the rest of the people of Belfast at security barriers where civilian searchers asked us to queue while they gave everyone a quick body search in order to prevent the IRA from getting bombs into the town. Standing beside the searchers were armed British soldiers. When we got to the main shops, Marks & Spencer, Boots and the local department stores such as Robinson & Cleaver or Anderson & McAuley, other searchers would be at the doors for another quick frisk and a glance into women's handbags and shopping bags.

Mum was an inveterate shopper and when I accompanied her I loved the lights, the newness and the fact that, in this environment, she was often at her happiest. She may have had money concerns but she didn't make them too obvious to us while we were young. I liked how, in this world, she seemed to revel in the possibilities that department stores offered. She would have audible discussions with herself about whether this blouse would go with the skirts she had or whether a size ten in Marksies was the same as a size ten in Primark. 'Cheap shops skimp on the material and two coats, which according to the labels are the same size, will fit very differently,' she told me, as if I was her best friend. Occasionally she saw things so nice she had to buy them for somebody – anybody. I think she liked to be complimented on her discerning taste and her eye for a bargain. She once told me to try on a shirt. As she saw me look at the label she said: 'Don't worry about the fact that it says Bust 32–34ins. That just means chest. It's for a girl but no one will know.'

The 'lemonade man' came into the street on Saturdays in his van, selling a variety of fizzy drinks. We sometimes got brown lemonade, white lemonade, American cream soda or the equally sweet-tasting Attaboy flavour. If Mum had enough money for ice cream we could make smokies – a lump of ice cream in a glass of lemonade.

Saturdays were also bath nights and Mum would run the water for us to have a bath, either together or consecutively, using the same bath water. She had an idiosyncratic concern about water that no one else I've ever met has shared. This concern was best observed on bath nights. 'We need something to soften the water,' she said to me. She produced a packet of Daz, her favourite soap powder. As I sat in the water, she would liberally sprinkle detergent in to 'soften' it. She did this on a regular basis and not as a one-off moment of madness. Once, she used Flash scouring powder. 'It's all the same,' she exclaimed in a tone that suggested any complaint would be met with an emphatic declaration of her authority in this matter. 'It's just detergent to make bubbles because that water's hard and needs to be softened. I'm not wasting money on bubble bath.' As she spoke, I could feel grains of soap powder that would remain solid under my bum and legs for several seconds before releasing their harsh cleaning power into the water. I'm not sure about producing a 'kind of bluey white you'll like', as the advertising claimed, but I do know that I have suffered dry skin, especially on my legs, since boyhood. Whether it was down to this unorthodox mothering, I'm not sure, but it can't have helped.

There was another more frightening incident in our bathroom that seemed to sum up the chaos that beset our home in the seventies. I arrived home from school at lunchtime to find Mum standing in the kitchen, making soup. I sat at the table and she gave me a bowl of soup and some bread. As Mum stood over by the cooker, a shot rang out. 'Jesus, Mary and Joseph!' she said, running by me through the living room and into the hall. The shot was clearly from inside the house. She raced upstairs and I followed right behind her. Unknown to me there was an IRA man upstairs. He was in the bathroom checking a pistol, a Colt 45 automatic, when it went off in his hand. The shot hit the tiles at the side of the bath, before it ricocheted down and took a large chunk of enamel off the edge of the bath exposing metal beneath.

'Are you OK? What are you doing?'

'It's OK, no problem,' said the man, regaining his composure.

Mum came out with her hand over her heart. 'Go on down and finish your lunch, Timothy,' she said. 'Don't be late for school.'

It wasn't the only near miss. Mum sometimes went on late-night cleaning sprees. One night while we were all in bed she began tidying the living room. With a cloth in her right hand, she wiped dust and dirt off the mantelpiece, collecting it in her left hand. Before she realised it, she had thrown not just the dirt but two bullets into a roaring fire. She carried on cleaning, and then she headed to the kitchen. As she did so the heat sent both bullets flying into the armchair opposite. Mum told us the tale the next day, laughing at her lucky escape.

After tea on Saturday evenings, while Bruce Forsyth was asking Anthea Redfern to 'Give us a twirl, darling', Mum was in the kitchen getting ready for her night out. This meant, for me, an endless series of orders to run up the stairs on fashion-related chores. 'Get me my black dress,' Mum would shout. I liked her assumption that I knew, as a ten-year-old boy, which dress she had in mind. 'Not that one, the other black one!' and I'd run off up the stairs again. I hated being the only boy in my class who knew anything about bras and the difference between shades of American Tan and Brandy tights.

With Mum asking 'What time is it?' every five minutes, I ran up getting her shoes. The black ones, of course. There were enough shoes, including many never worn, for her to open a small boutique. 'Get me the black shoes that I wore to the wedding, when your aunt Kathleen was drunk. The ones that I wore with that grey, knee-length dress. They have a high heel but not those slingbacks and they're not court shoes. There's a strap across the top and an open toe.' None the wiser, I sprinted upstairs and grabbed every pair of black shoes I could find and brought them down. This was preferable to getting it wrong, even though I'd have to carry them all back up again and very, very carefully, throw them in a sprawling, indiscriminate mess under her bed until the following week.

Occasionally my heart would sink when I realised that two potential sources of unmitigated disaster had yet to be confronted. Firstly, in the days before central heating, I had to make sure that there was enough hot water for Mum to have a bath. If I was on top of my game, I had already put a pressure cooker and the kettle on to boil water for the inevitable 'top ups'. Then, after her bath, Mum would storm downstairs and across the living room floor in various states of undress to get ready in the kitchen, thereby maximising disruption to the rest of us. We always used the back door so on a Saturday we were effectively walking through her changing room. 'Get out! Get out!' she would scream, crouching at the sink as my friends and I arrived at the back door.

I eventually learned to tell my mates to wait at the front gate. This was especially important when I learned that among the last items my mum would decide on wearing were her bra and knickers. 'Run up and get me a bra,' she would say. As I raced up the stairs I could hear her shouting, 'The black one. The *new* black one.' I knew that clearing the drawer of all black underwear and carrying it to her was the only way to get it right. She knew that too and would laugh when I walked back into the kitchen looking like an explosion in a lingerie shop.

It would be nice if memories of my role in Mum's nights out ended when I reached puberty, but this little intimacy continued until the year she died. And while I romanticise a ritual I didn't always care for, I did always like it when she asked me to zip up the back of her dress. This meant she was almost ready and the shouting and errand-running was almost over. It also meant that I witnessed at close quarters Mum becoming 'Going Out Mum'. I knew that she would then go into the living room, have a drink and wait for her taxi to arrive. She was ready to sparkle and I could relax with my brothers watching *Starsky and Hutch* and *Match of the Day* with my Kola Kubes and a tin of Coke.

Young, Lifted and Black

Our family had been involved in the armed struggle for long enough that even the Belfast Brigade of the IRA now considered our house anything but safe. Many safe houses eventually were overused and Mum was glad to be left in peace. The IRA might have gone away, more or less, but the Brits still dropped in for their 4 a.m. raids. 'Those boys have to go to school. You're not taking them out of their beds. They need their sleep,' Mum shouted, as soldiers flooded the house again. There was an element of jaded ritual about it all. Soldiers entered our bedrooms despite Mum's concerns. One lifted up the mattress at Paddy's side of our double bed, sending him tumbling down towards me and squashing both of us between the wall and the mattress. 'Clear!' he shouted, peering through the bedstead to the fluff-covered old shoes, *Dandy* annuals and bits of the Monopoly board game below.

Due to my delayed entry into primary school there were problems when it came time to transfer to secondary school. In an attempt to remedy the situation I was given the chance to sit the 11 Plus with other children of my age, but hardly in ideal conditions. For one hour a day, while I was in primary six, I was taken from my class to a primary seven class to sit among boys I was not familiar with to study mock test papers. At the end of each session, I was sent back to my own class. This went on for a few weeks leading up to the test. I failed. And, at the end of primary six, instead of going naturally on to primary seven, I was sent straight to St Paul's Secondary School.

I was extremely nervous about joining secondary school even though I knew that the school was only about five hundred yards from the back of my house. Overnight, I moved from being one of the oldest boys in my class to being one of the youngest. I was petrified of having my head shoved down the toilet, a regular initiation for First Years. I worried, too, that I would stand out as an obvious target – the Brits had taught me that lesson many times. I made sure I went to the toilets as little as possible and even sprinted home at break times just so I could have a pee. Sometimes I waited until class started and went when the corridors were empty.

In my five years there I never set foot in the canteen for the same reason. The older boys threw food, soup, custard and fruit at the First Years. They even threw First Years. So I went home for lunch. She often worked, and we had to open tins of soup. Mum would sometimes make rice pudding and leave it to simmer. As an extra treat she sprinkled raisins in it or squeezed in some orange juice to add more flavour. We helped ourselves to the Penguin biscuits she set out for us.

Mum was a great cook and often asked for feedback on what we thought of the Sunday dinner, or if we had noticed that she had switched to new potatoes. She loved to bake cakes and would ask if we preferred our apple cakes with or without cinnamon flavouring. She would cut oranges into slices for us to eat but, as our grabbing hands reached to get the biggest slices, she would tell us to wait before liberally sprinkling sugar on them. Mum wanted to give us the best – this was her way of improving on what Mother Nature had provided.

Depending on how late Mum was for work, the house might still smell of her hairspray or perfume. Hairbrushes, hair rollers, coats, skirts and shoes were strewn from the kitchen sink in a raggle-taggle trail across the floor, through the door and right across the living room, as Mum, running late and panicking, sprinted out the front door at around eleven thirty each morning. She started work at eleven. If I stood still in the living room at lunchtime, it was almost possible to hear her 'Jesus, Mary and Josephs' and her 'I'm sick of its...' as she realised that, yet again, she was late. Her stress hung in the air long after she had gone.

My first year established me as reasonably sporty and I had no real fears once people got used to me. I would get tense passing lines of older boys in the corridor. I half-anticipated either direct name-calling or a mumble and then a loud laugh as someone made a comment. This daily feeling made me drop my head and avoid eye contact in case someone took this to be provocation on my part. However, despite my fears, I was never bullied in any systematic way or by any one person or gang. My distress, when it did occur, was at feeling wounded or exposed by comments and 'jokes'. I never had a comeback.

One boy, Martin George, or 'Georgie', was physically much bigger than the rest of us and, on the first day of the first class, he looked around and pointed his pen at boys in turn.

'Name?'

'What?'

'What's your name?'

'Campbell.'

'You're "Soupy"!'

'You?'

'Scott.'

'You can be "Scotty".'

Everyone had a nickname or a slagging name: 'Flea', 'Fatso', 'Ginger Nut', 'Squinty', 'Onion', 'Mackers'. My school chums and friends from my street never called me any racist names. Instead, they used to slag me with a very humdrum term they settled on when they heard about a domestic mishap I had one evening when I accidentally put vinegar in my tea instead of sprinkling it over my chips. I was therefore referred to as 'Salt and Vinegar'. This, I thought, was fair because I didn't really think it was on for me to call someone with red hair 'Ginger Nut' only to hear them call me 'nigger' in response. That would have been disproportionate. I just prayed that the entire class would observe this rule and during our five years together they did. It was actually quite enlightened thinking. One boy in Thursday afternoon English class audibly asked: 'Why don't we just call him "nigger"?' He was shushed by some others in the class. The word 'him' hurt me as much as the word 'nigger', as I was being referred to in the third person. It had a 'them and us' quality to it and singled me out when I wanted to fit in. 'I'm just like you,' I thought.

No one had heard of political correctness in those days. In fact, I was living in a world where racism was part of the main TV schedules in sitcoms such as *Mind Your Language* and *Love Thy Neighbour*. The racist 'comics' who appeared every night on a show called *The Comedians* also caused me discomfort as they gave people lots of one-liners. I hated their powder-blue suits, dickie-bow ties and vicious prejudices. Their one-liners were often repeated to me by people the next day; sometimes a 'No offence, Tim' followed the jokes, sometimes not.

The odious Jim Davison and his comedy character, 'Chalkie', so-called because chalk is white and he was – wait for it – *black*, was the nadir. Such crude thinking meant that I often heard people impersonating Davison's cod West Indian accent. They would shout his trademark catchphrase, 'Oooo-kaaay' at me. No other words needed to be said for this to be a putdown and a humiliation.

When Lenny Henry came along towards the end of my schooldays, he wasn't much better. One of his comic creations was an African character and therefore wore leopard-skin loin-cloths, headbands and lion's-tooth necklaces. I hated his stupid outfit and his stupid catchphrase 'Katanga!' which inevitably some kids shouted at me in the street or the school corridor.

Even when a programme did portray black people in a more positive light, people still found ways of making it the basis for racist remarks. While I was a schoolboy, the mini-series *Roots*, about Africans being kidnapped to serve as slaves in the United States, was broadcast. The epic show depicted one American black man's journey to discover his family's African ancestry and was, ultimately, an uplifting melodrama with the triumph of the human spirit over adversity and racial bigotry as its message. Or at least, it was meant to be positive; it wasn't for me. While I enjoyed watching it, I had to get used to kids in my school, in the area and, of course, soldiers in the ubiquitous British Army patrols calling me 'Kunta' or 'Kunta Kinte', the name of the main character in the show. 'Your name is Toby! Say your name!' they said, directly quoting an unforgettable scene in which Kunta Kinte is brutally and repeatedly whipped until he accepts his slave name.

Each spring, we had to raise money for 'the missions' during the six weeks of Lent. I wasn't really sure what the missions were or how they helped. One morning the teacher said, 'The black babies are little orphans in Africa and the Catholic Church and all of us are going to help them. Every Lent, we collect money for them. You have to sell ballots in your area.' The class sat silent. Boys glanced around in my direction.

'Is Brannigan a black baby, sir?'

'Are you adopted, Tim?'

'What about white babies, sir? Why don't we give them the money?'

'What country are you from, Tim?'

'Can you speak oola boola language, Tim?'

'Shut up, you! Ignore him, Tim, he's an eejit.'

'What? I'm just askin'.'

'Call him "honky", Tim.'

'Only slagging, Tim,' they said.

Our teachers decided to set up a league of all the first-year classes to see which class could raise the most money for the 'black babies'. Our teacher, Mr Tohill, was extremely enthusiastic and made no secret of his desire to out perform his colleagues by winning trophies and raising money for the orphans and the starving children. He bragged about us in the staff room. We responded to his enthusiasm and not only won all the sporting trophies but raised the most money of any class in our year.

In my third year, I was horrified when two black boys, brothers I think, came to our school from Manchester. Until their arrival, I was relatively secure in my only-black-kid-in-town role. Now, I was afraid that my colour would become an issue. Most of the boys in school seemed to take the arrival of other black kids in their stride but a vocal few made comments. A day or two after the brothers arrived, I was moving from one class to another and, as I headed up the stairs to the top floor, the two boys passed going the other way. I heard a boy say to his mate: 'There's three of them, now.' Again, I had been moved from being one of us – part of the gang – to one of *them*, an outsider, and there was nothing I could do about it. When I moved around the school I was anxious that I might run into the brothers and relief and delight, as well as a little guilt, were my overwhelming emotions when they moved on after only a few months.

I relished my freedoms at St Paul's although not the schoolwork. I never went 'on the beak', as we called playing truant. However, there were frustrations. One September morning we lined up in the middle corridor to wait to go into class on the first day of a new school year. A maths teacher, who used to enjoy slagging us, looked us up and down and said loudly, 'Well, I see Brannigan's been away somewhere warm again.'

I underachieved at school and had been distracted by among other things, the mod revival that occurred around that time. *Quadrophenia* was the cult movie. We wore parkas, desert boots and boating jackets. Mum was livid when I failed to make it into the CSE class at the beginning of fourth year. An unwillingness to apply myself, especially to subjects I didn't like, was to blame. The changing demographics of Belfast led to falling numbers in my school, which meant that in my third year the authorities decided that instead of two classes, some sixty pupils, being allowed to study at CSE level, there would be only one class of thirty pupils. I missed the cut.

When I got home, Mum followed me into the hall and asked what class I would be in when fourth year started. I kept walking up the stairs as I told her I wouldn't be in the top class. 'I'll mod you,' she said as she grabbed me by the fishtail of my green parka coat and pulled me down towards her. I was near the top of our stairs at the time, so I fell backwards and almost on top of her. I grabbed the banister and managed to break my fall, otherwise I would have tumbled down into the hall, possibly taking Mum with me. When I got up she grabbed me by the lapels, shouting constantly. I was told that I'd better 'smarten up'. Mum couldn't understand why I was described as being 'too talkative' and 'too giddy' in school reports. She couldn't fathom why her most obedient son suddenly became this chattering boy at school. Five out of ten teachers mentioned my talking on one report. 'Tim is bright and lively but talks too much,' wrote one. 'D – capable of much better but won't stop talking,' read another.

She grabbed me by the face with one hand, her thumb pressing into my right cheek, her fingers grabbing my left. I was pinned to the wall. 'What are you talking about in school all day? What? Tell me!'

I had no answer. Lying on my bed, I wondered why my brothers didn't get this treatment. They felt the force of Mum's temper but certainly not to the same extent. I knew their exam results were nothing special and they were allowed to lie in and take days off. In retrospect, I can see that Mum's expect-ations for me were driven by the fact that my father was academically and financially successful. But at the time I resented these moods; her temper, her constant shouting and her double standards. Being out of Mum's sphere of influence and unrelenting discipline allowed me to rebel and get boisterous whether in the street or in school. The more expans-ive side of my character came to the fore. My closest friends seemed to have very different relationships with their parents. They made demands; they talked over TV programmes and argued with each other during the news. They enjoyed the luxury of answering back when their parents spoke to them. This was a revelation to me.

When she was pregnant with me Mum had been adamant that as a well-paid doctor Michael should provide as good an education for their son as he was doing for the children he already had with his wife. Why should her son not have the same opportunities as his other children? She did not ask for money for herself, but simply that he provide for me to attend a better standard of school than was likely to be available to me. Although Michael had promised he would do this he never contributed financially to my upbringing.

The late seventies were a real low point for us. Mum was up to her eyes in debt – I often had holes in my shoes and usually only had one pair at a time and I wore hand-me-down clothes, including a green snorkel jacket with a busted zip. There were other humiliations. One wet, gusty Saturday evening, a gale tore Mum's large bedroom window from its hinges and flung it into the street. As we came out to the front of the house to see what had happened, neighbours looked on from behind their newly fitted, fancier windows. I was angry but said nothing. This was one family disaster that only Mum could be blamed for. She loved to sleep in bed with the window open as wide as possible to get 'plenty of air' about the room. And the kissing couple that leaned against our crumbling garden wall in the heat of a passionate embrace must have been shocked when a large section of brickwork and railings gave way and they landed in a garden filled with long grass, weeds and crisp packets. These were desperate times.

By the early eighties things were looking up. Mum went back to work, taking on various bar and restaurant jobs. She also had help from Chris who would contribute to the family income with money from his driving jobs, although he was the victim of some reasonably lengthy periods of unemployment. Ciaran and Paul chipped in too, but perhaps their moving on – Ciaran to married life and Paul to live in Australia – was the biggest help in terms of creating a bit more space and giving her two less mouths to feed at home.

In 1982 Mum took Paddy and me to Majorca. The holiday was one of a number of indicators that suggested we were slowly starting to get our heads above water. Mum got a second-hand washing machine, meaning no more washing by hand, and a new (to us) green bathroom suite replaced the one that had been damaged when the gun went off. Best of all, we got central heating. We had a phone installed which delighted Mum, at least until the bills arrived. And she clapped her hands in an approving and excited way when she heard that not one but two Chinese restaurants were to open in the area. 'Can you believe it, love? Chinese restaurants in Beechmount?' She read too much into the word 'restaurant' – fast food bars would have been a more accurate term. Mum's hopes of walking into a beautiful restaurant to be greeted by a polite and refined maître d' never materialised. One of the 'restaurants' was soon dubbed 'Provie Charlie's'.

The first IRA hunger strike was called off as it reached crisis point in late 1980. The IRA was discovered that the deal they had struck with the British government was a sham. A second hunger strike, led by Bobby Sands, got underway in March 1981. Mum made me attend the first march in support of the hunger strikes even though I wanted to watch Brian Moore commentate on ITV's *The Big Match*.

'Are you going to the march, Timothy?' Mum asked.

'I was going to watch the football.'

'Men are going to die – get round to that march!' And right there another of our discussions ended.

I attended alone. The crowd moved at glacial speed along

the Falls Road. The numbers overwhelmed me. I stood on boulders outside an off-licence for a view, instantly hooked on the fate of the hunger strikers and their leader, Bobby Sands. The seventies were gone but much of the crowd seemed stuck in a time warp. Despite The Sex Pistols and punk, despite The Clash, David Bowie's 'Ashes to Ashes' and New Wave, this throng wore their snorkel coats with pride. The wide lapels of sports jackets flapped defiantly. People dressed in flared trousers without attempting to be ironic. With their old clothes, old hairstyles, and old politics, they were like hippies in a land where it was easier to lay your hands on a bomb than a bong. It was the first of many, many marches and the crowd walked in silence, their uncertain speculation about winning muffled by duffle coats and beards. There may have been flute bands. I don't recall them. I just remember a silent, deathly hush.

We became news junkies, watching and listening to every hourly bulletin. The entire country was on deathwatch. As teenagers, our street-corner chat was strewn with evidence of a new vocabulary: negotiations, commissions, rallies, speakers, pleas, delegations, interventions, intransigence, emissaries, Red Cross, European Commission of Human Rights, Thatcher, reneged, questions in the House. 'A crime is a crime is a crime,' Thatcher said. The hunger strike was the IRA's 'last card', she claimed and she would not give in to terrorists.

I began attending marches either alone or with friends. The H-block hunger strike was heading towards a critical moment. Sands was nearing death and Thatcher would not give in – we couldn't believe she would let him die. I joined Youth Against H-blocks and heard people speak about mobilising our youth.

Just after 1 a.m. on 5 May 1981, days before my fifteenth birthday, Bobby Sands died. Ireland erupted. I went down to the Falls Road the next day and found that the local bank had been burned out and intense rioting meant that many vehicles burned overnight were reduced to smouldering shells of metal sunk in beds of ash and cinders. There were barricades across the Falls Road but mainly they were across Beechmount Avenue making it difficult, if not impossible, to enter the area in a vehicle. I'd never seen anything like it. I was living in a war zone. Many of the rioters had gone home exhausted and the Brits had returned to their barracks, probably for the same reason. A father and son had been killed when rioters tried to hijack their milk float over in north Belfast. Some people were still milling around, angry that Bobby Sands had died and swapping tales of petrol bombing the Brits. I was angry that I'd slept through it all. At about 11 a.m. I returned to the house and started to make some breakfast. Mum was still in bed and I went up to offer her some breakfast. She asked what time it was and then, as I feared, she asked, 'Why are you not at school, Timothy?'

'I went down to the front of the road. Bobby Sands has died and there's burned out cars everywhere.'

'And what has that got to do with you going to school?'

I didn't reply. Her rhetorical tone meant she was angry.

'Get your uniform on and get to school!'

I went to school to find that about two thirds of the class had stayed off. The rest of us sat around like it was the last day of term. Teachers, some of whom lived in areas away from the riots, asked us what we had seen. About noon, the classroom door opened suddenly and an IRA man, whom I recognised instantly, stood in the doorway with the snorkel-style hood of his coat pulled up to cover his face. 'Get out, now!' he said before running down the corridor repeating the message at each classroom. 'Don't listen to that idiot,' said our teacher dismissively, sparking a discussion about the armed struggle and the IRA.

On 12 May just after 6 p.m. I was at my friend Kevin McCausland's house across the street. 'Francis Hughes has just died on hunger strike. It was on the news,' I told him. When I met up with Kevin the next day it was his turn to have shocking news – the Pope had been shot, he told me. This was too much. I ran home to tell Mum.

'Who told you that?'

'Kevin.'

'What would he know? Don't be stupid. Do you believe everything you hear?'

Some weeks later, Kevin and I made the long trek up to the Lenadoon estate in west Belfast. Another man, Joe McDonnell, had died on hunger strike. His body lay in state in his living room and we went up to pay our respects, but mostly we were drawn out of morbid curiosity as young boys. I was stunned by the crowds as we approached the house. As we got to the gate, several IRA men came out of the house wearing their uniforms. They looked fantastic, like real soldiers. They wore masks and dark glasses. We walked into the living room, pretended to say a prayer and stared at the two IRA volunteers standing to attention. They looked like gods. We enjoyed the long walk home, talking breathlessly about what we had just seen.

'The IRA looked class, didn't they?'

'Fucking magic – did you see their uniforms?'

'One of them looked right at me when I was beside the coffin.'

'I was looking to see if they had guns? Did you see a gun?'

'No, but they probably had some.'

We both attended Joe McDonnell's funeral. I had been at Bobby Sands' funeral but was disappointed that, with the crowds being so big, I couldn't get near the graveside. I asked someone when the IRA would fire shots over the coffin and a man told me that he believed that it had happened further up the road as the cortege had made its way towards the cemetery. For the McDonnell funeral, we got ourselves placed by the point where we knew the IRA firing party would come out. The coffin was set on trestles in the middle of the road. The world's press were on one side of the coffin; the IRA with their rifles was on the other. As the volleys of shots rang out the empty shells bounced around the ground by and underneath the coffin. I was among many mourners who lurched forward, trying to grab one as a souvenir.

The hunger strikes came to an end on 3 October 1981, having been broken by the prisoners' families intervening as each of the men slipped into a coma. They asked for medical attention on behalf of their sons and several men, close to death, were taken off the strike. The sense of chaos diminished as the weeks and months went by and the rallies got smaller. By the time the tenth hunger striker died, I noticed there wasn't even rioting in Beechmount.

I had attended the first rally in support of the hunger strikers, I went to several of the funerals and I attended what I believe was the last march, after the ten men had died. Throughout that summer and autumn we had 'Support the Hunger Strikers' posters in our living room windows. Paddy and I made sure to hang out the black flag with each death. The final march took place on a rain-lashed night in Ballymurphy, a mile from my home. It was attended by several hundred people as opposed to the many thousands who had been there at the start. I was proud still to be attending marches in the dark, wet winter nights. The speaker spent as much time talking about Sinn Féin's 'potential' were they to stand for election as he did about the hunger strikers. Republicans were normally opposed to, or at best ambivalent about, electoral politics. We feared being 'seduced into the State', losing our revolutionary status. We feared becoming reformist and conformist when we were actual revolutionaries. But the international media and political attention Sinn Féin experienced when Bobby Sands stood for, and was elected to, Westminster while he was halfway through his hunger strike proved tantalising. It allowed the movement to demonstrate that they were more than a small band of terrorists with no support in the community.

My fifth-year exams approached. In the back bedroom of our house one Thursday evening, I wrote a poem as part of my school coursework. My poem was around seven or eight verses long and warned the reader of the dangers of smoking. I wrote it in one sitting and presented it the next day. My teacher read it, held it up above her head and said, 'Brannigan, stand up. Did you write this?'

'Yes, miss.'

'When?'

'Last night.'

'No, you didn't!' She was incredulous. 'How long did it take you?'

'Don't know. An hour? Not long, miss. Why do you think I didn't write it, miss?'

'Did someone help you?'

'No.'

'But it rhymes all the way through,' she looked at me. And *no one* helped you? *No one?*'

Without answering her final question, I looked at her and sat down. I knew that people would be thinking that I had cheated.

We didn't stand a chance at school. It was as if when the bell rang at 9 a.m. it was a cue to some teachers to start undermining the fragile confidence of pupils in their charge. Even when we made the effort we were viewed suspiciously by some of the teachers with their middle-class pretensions and their finely honed prejudices.

Mum kept up the pressure over schoolwork and at weekends would ask me if I'd done my homework. 'Go and get me your exercise books!'

'Look at the state of that writing.' She threw the book back at me. 'Write that out again and do it neatly. Your best handwriting – and stop your tutting or I'll tut you.'

My final exam results were extremely disappointing, given my potential. Mum became hysterical. Pleas for her to 'calm down' only seemed to induce increased states of frenzy. My strategy veered between arguing my corner (but not too forcefully) and simply adopting a stance of stoic silence until the storm passed. 'You'll be going back to school, do you hear me?'

she shouted. Her tone suggested that this was a threat. I certainly took it as one.

My world was changing. The comfort zone of school was slipping away and the adult world of work and responsibilities started to occupy my thoughts. I lacked confidence and I worried about discrimination and how people would react to me, as a black teenager, at job interviews.

Mum made me attend an open night for young people in west Belfast where careers advisors and representatives of local businesses had little stalls, leaflets and other literature to give out. The event was at a school on the Glen Road in Andersonstown, some distance from my home. I had no memory of ever having been on that road except in a car when we went to a relative's house. I walked all the way up after a heated discussion with Mum about the merits of the exercise. When I got to the Glen Road I realised that I didn't know where the school was. It was dark and I wandered up the fairly deserted road. In the distance I saw an elderly woman coming towards me. Between us was a line of large, mature trees, the trunks of which were massive. 'Excuse me,' I shouted. 'Can you tell me where St Mary's...'

I could see the woman hesitate. I moved from one side of the large tree to the other trying to see her. 'Can you tell me where...' The trees got in the way again. She presumably thought I was using the trees as cover.

'Help! Help me somebody!'

'You're OK, I'm just looking for...'

'Help! He's trying to attack me!' She shouted to two young men on the other side of the road. I was as scared as she was. I stopped and stood with my arms outstretched as the young lads came towards me. They seemed about my age.

'What's wrong, love?'

'He's going to attack me.'

'I'm not. I'm lost. I'm just trying to find the school,' I said, pleading.

'What school?' one of the lads asked.

'St Mary's. I'm just going to a careers night.'

'It's just over there, on the other side.'

I thanked him and crossed the road. It made me realise that even when I felt nervous and lost, to others I still represented a threat. I was still a potential mugger or rapist. It could have been much worse if the lads who came to the old woman's aid had been more belligerent.

Many friends from school were no longer around; some got jobs, others signed on. A friend from my street had a can of spray paint. We wrote our names on a wall on the Falls Road. I told him to keep a lookout for any RUC Land Rovers as I wrote my name and the phrase 'Class of '82' as well as the names of some friends from my class. No Land Rovers came but an unmarked car carrying two RUC men pulled up and we were arrested. Mum was annoyed but calmed down very quickly when I was released from the police barracks.

'Why did you write Class of '82?' she asked.

'I don't know. I liked school and now all my friends have gone.'

There was a pause as she considered this and then she said, 'Don't ever write on walls again.'

In the last week of my school days in spring 1982 Mum told me that she had applied for some jobs on my behalf and had lined up two interviews. One was in a barber's shop in town; the other, two days later, was in the biggest hairdressing salon in the city centre, Michele International. Mum never stopped repeating the mantra: 'You should always have a trade to fall back on.' I didn't go to the barber's shop interview. I was too nervous. Often, simply leaving the comfort zone of Beechmount made me apprehensive. I was also painfully shy. I'm not sure Mum ever realised how vulnerable I felt to the racist comments that were a frequent feature of my youth. She demanded that I attend the second interview. After passing the salon several times – I was intimidated by the smoked-glass window, the display-case lit with spotlights and the glamorous, peroxide-blonde receptionist – I ventured in for my interview with the owner. I was stunned by the size of the place and it transpired that there was only one man among some thirty-five staff. It was so busy I could hardly take anything in. Glamorous-looking staff smiled as they passed me and I was delighted to be told that I should start work on Monday. I was not a natural hairdresser, although I learned a lot of social skills and enjoyed chatting with the girls. I knew that I would eventually go back to college to do my A levels, so even as I washed, cut and styled hair, I also attended night classes to get some CSEs.

I was quite radicalised by the mid-1980s. On May Day 1984, I joined Sinn Féin. I had been a de facto member for some years as I had begun selling the party's weekly newspaper *Republican News* during the hunger strike. Along with other members in the Mid-Falls Sinn Féin area, I tramped the streets every Thursday or Friday night selling copies of the paper door to door. It was slow, long, thankless political work. In the 1980s, many young people, including a close friend of mine, saw the radicalism of the IRA as infinitely preferable to the slow, mundane work of building a political base. I did feel some pressure to join the IRA, not because anyone tried to persuade me, but rather because people I knew, and one close friend in particular, were taking much bigger risks than I was. He never said much to me explicitly but he suddenly became unaccountably busy or had to go to 'meetings'. Selling newspapers and putting up election posters seemed tame by comparison.

My increasingly left-wing politics were responsible for me losing my job at the salon. Towards the end of my three-year apprenticeship, I decided I'd had enough of the low wages that are standard in the hairdressing industry and spoke to the Transport and General Workers' Union. I went to the union's headquarters and was given forty membership forms to distribute among the staff. I had to get all the girls to act in concert on the same day so that no one stuck their neck out and found themselves isolated. I gave everyone a membership form and asked them to fill them in and return them to me the following morning so that I could get them back to the union rep. When I got to work the next day, the staff room smelled of burning paper. The management had found out about my plans because one girl, a 'firm's woman' had told them what I was doing. 'I'm happy with my wages, Tim. Sorry' said a senior stylist.

'Me too,' said another.

'If you don't go through with this, I'm out of here. I'll be sacked.' Lots of people stared at the floor – the moment was lost. When I completed my apprenticeship I was politely but firmly shown the door. I was due to leave anyway to go back to college so I didn't mind too much. Still, it was a valuable lesson about the world of work.

As I left the hairdressers, the owner of the salon handed me a letter and, in a jocular way, said, 'When I read this letter I just knew I had to give you a job! It's the letter your mum wrote to me asking if I would employ you. I promised myself I'd keep it to embarrass you on the day you were leaving.'

Written on thin blue Basildon Bond writing paper, it was typical of Mum. As I recall, there was nothing in the letter about my skills, my love of hairdressing, or my aptitude for the work. Instead, Mum made it seem like she was doing the world of hairdressing in general, and Michele's salon in particular, a big favour: 'My son, Timothy, is studying for his exams at the moment. If you were to offer him a job in your beautiful salon, I would consider allowing him to give up his studies to work for you. He is a lovely boy with beautiful coffee-coloured skin ...'

I gave Mum the letter when I got home from work. She reacted badly to it and was inexplicably angry. She told me later that the letter made her realise that I was growing up fast and that she wouldn't always be around to smooth my way in the world. It also made her realise that maybe it was time to tell me about my father.

Mum's Secret is Out

I will never forget the day I learned the truth about the circumstances surrounding my birth; it was the day before Live Aid – Friday 12 July 1985. Some of my aunts, uncles and cousins decided to have a bit of a party in my uncle's holiday home in the small seaside village of Cushendall on the County Antrim coast. We were observing the time-honoured tradition of nationalists in the north who fled Belfast and other towns to avoid the thousands of Orangemen marching around in their sashes, bowler hats and white gloves. Cushendall offered us stunning views of the mountains, the sea and cosy bars. It also spared us the indignity of having local ITV and BBC tell us that the sectarianism and religious fundamentalism expressed in speeches by members of the Orange Order had a carnival atmosphere about it. The Brethren, as they quaintly referred to themselves, applauded dire warnings about 'papist plots' and 'republican rebels' and, for a while, it must have seemed to them, in their seventeenth-century idyll, that all was right with the world.

I went along to the Brennan clan soirée on the understanding that Mum, Chris and I would all be back home in time for the Live Aid concert from Wembley which was to begin around noon the following day. However, only hours before Status Quo started rocking all over the world, my own world was shaken to its core by Mum's spontaneous decision to let me into her secret. We'd had a few drinks and there was a cosy atmosphere. We had been chatting about my future plans and she was delighted to hear that I wanted to get a degree and then go on to become a journalist.

'Journalism would be great; you could travel and meet people from other countries. I'd love to see you going to other countries. Do you not want to see something better than Belfast and all of our troubles? I'm not saying you should ignore the Troubles – always know what you believe in – but you should travel.' And then, out of the blue, she shocked me. 'Timothy, love, I've something to tell you. I'm your real mum and you are my son. You're not adopted.'

Irish families are littered with young men and women who have been shocked to find that 'Mum' isn't really Mum and that much of what they believed to be true was a lie. Now, I was being told that the woman I called Mum really was my mother; not a kind-hearted soul who took pity on me in an orphanage but my real, honest-to-goodness, flesh-and-blood mother. I was nineteen, now was as good a time as any to tell me. A crowded party it may have been but Mum was more likely to be talkative in a relaxed late-night setting than in the cold light of day. And of course she had been drinking which freed her of any inhibitions: 'I've already told you that your father was a doctor but I should tell you all about him some day. But that's another wee story.'

'That's another wee story' was an important coda for Mum. It meant that she was in the mood to keep talking about a point, or would do so if encouraged. She seemed a bit unsure of how much she should tell me. She seemed to be at her most approachable, most agreeable best. Mum could handle her drink and was almost always a warmer, shimmering, effervescent version of herself with a glass in her hand. She was a natural storyteller, too. I pressed her on this revelation.

'Tell me about my father. Tell me that wee story, then,' I said. Mum had often told me my father was a doctor, as if this was a guarantee of quality, decency and integrity.

This was her night, her moment, her story and after

almost twenty years, finally, she was ready to tell it.

'I've been meaning to tell you this for ages. I was always worried about when the right time would be. Do you think this is the right time? Do you want to hear this now, love?'

'Yes, of course. Why not?'

'OK. You won't be angry, will you?'

'No.' I was slightly anxious as I was wondering what she was talking about and what the drama could be. I was intrigued more than anything. She began talking about a dance hall she went to with friends in 1965.

'Your father came over to us. He was gorgeous, big and tall. He asked us – I can't remember if he singled any one out in particular – if one of us wanted to dance.'

Mum's friend, not used to being around black men, had run behind the other women, trying to hide. 'She called your father a "nigger". I was furious at her,' Mum said. 'He walked away again.'

I didn't say much and didn't ask questions. I just looked at her, nodded and let her continue. She told me how she plucked up the courage to speak to my father.

'So, anyway, when Ladies' Choice came, I walked over to him and asked if he would like to dance and that was that really...'

'Well, there had to be more than that, Mum.'

'What? Oh, yes, well we had an affair but it was very brief. He lived on the Malone road and I used to meet him, sometimes in town and sometimes on the front of the road, at the Broadway Picture House, usually.'

'Mum! That was a bit close to home.'

'I know. And, before I knew it, I was pregnant. I couldn't believe it,' she said, her voice trailing off.

'God! What did you do?'

'Well, I told your father: "I'm pregnant," I said. And he said, "I'm married". His wife was an eye-specialist from Nigeria, I think. He didn't want to know. "We can get rid of it", he said'.

'So then what happened?'

'Oh, love. I was sick with worry from the start because I knew the baby wasn't Tom's. I knew you were going to be black and I knew I wasn't going to do what your father wanted me to do – "get rid of it".' She changed her tone of voice, to make it clear that this was his phrase, not hers. She did not agree with abortion.

'I asked him to help me but he backed off most of the time. Sometimes he got in touch.'

'What did he want?'

'What do men always want? He was after one thing ...'

Mum explained that he promised to pay for the weekly upkeep in the baby home and to make sure that I got a 'good education', but he never did. 'That was all I asked of him,' she said. 'He made promises and didn't keep them.'

Mum also told me she believed that my father had got at least one other Belfast woman pregnant. 'Even when I was heavily pregnant with you I saw him walk into a bar with another man and they had women with them. A woman was linking your father's arm. It looked to me as if they were out on a date.'

This was a lot of information to take on board. Mum made me promise not to tell anyone – she wanted to tell her brothers and children herself. I had a lot of questions. 'How did you get away with it? How did people not know? When I was born people would have seen that I was black. And if you put me in the home then people must have asked what happened to me. It doesn't make sense. You went in to hospital to have a baby and then what happened?'

She told me about her plan and the fake death story.

'I just told people you were adopted after I brought you home from St Joseph's. People thought you were adopted and that was it as far as I was concerned.'

'I thought I was adopted too, Mum,' I said laughing.

Mum laughed.

'Are you annoyed, love?'

'Not at all, are you serious? It's an amazing story. The

doctors and nurses must have compromised their ethics and standards.' Mum raised her eyebrows and bit her lip, suggesting that she had never actually considered that crucial point in all of the drama. Eventually she asked: 'Are you sure you're OK? I wasn't going to leave you in the home. I just had to come up with a plan to get you out of there.' It sounded like she was still defending her actions two decades later. She needn't have bothered.

'It must have been very difficult for you – a lot of stress.'

'I couldn't sleep, love. Every day I worried about what would happen, what my mother would say. Your granda was very religious. I worried about your future and I wanted you to know who your father was. That's why you have the middle name Ekue. That was your father's surname.' As a child she had told me about the name Ekue, but because I believed I was adopted and had little interest in tracking my father down I never asked further questions.

'The doctors wanted me to give you an ordinary name but I was determined you would know about your African heritage. Your father's from Ghana. They told me it would be cruel to give you an African name – you were so light they said. I wanted you to have your father's name and I said I wouldn't change my mind … Why are you crying, Timothy?'

'Because I'm happy,' I said.

'Well, could you smile or something? People are looking over at us,' she joked.

I looked around and my uncle Vivian was observing us from afar. He knew that Mum and I sometimes had a difficult relationship.

Mum was drinking vodka and coke. With her left hand cradling the bottom of the glass, she ran her finger around the top edge of it. She often held any glass or cup in this way. When drinking tea, she would often try to read the tea leaves. She didn't really know how to do this; she just looked for shapes and patterns. She liked notions of higher beings, God and supernatural influences. At its most basic level, she thought there was something in the maxim: 'What goes around comes around'.

'What did Tom say about all of this? What did you tell him?'

She put her hand over her mouth, her eyebrows arched.

'I don't know what I told him … I told him something … Did I? I think so.'

'He didn't walk out, though?'

'No!' She leaned forward and whispered even more conspiratorially. 'No, he didn't and he could have, so no matter what else I say about him, you should always give him respect for that. He could have used you as an excuse to leave us but he didn't.'

'Does Ciaran know any of this?' I asked.

'Why Ciaran?' her voice quickened, as if she sensed danger.

'I'm just asking because he was the eldest. He would remember all of this.'

'No, I've never told him and I don't want you to. I've no idea how he would react but it wouldn't be good, so don't tell him. I'll tell them all in my own good time, in my own way. Don't tell anyone.'

As the evening wore on, other people began to intrude into our corner and we had to keep changing the subject. We finished with Mum saying that she knew she was very strict with me but that she didn't want me to be stuck in a dead-end job. She spoke in an apologetic tone. 'I want you to be successful and go and meet your father to show him what you have done. I want your father to be proud of you. Will you look for him? I think he might be in London. I want him to be able to see how you are and that you were raised well. That's why I don't want you being cheeky or answering back or saying "aye" instead of "yes". I know I've been hard on you but I just want the best for you, love; something better than Belfast and the Troubles. I'm delighted you want to be a journalist. Now work hard for your A levels.' I hoped that now she had told me the truth she might not have to be so uptight with me. I hoped it would lead to a more relaxed relationship between us.

We talked about whether I should live in a more cosmopolitan city, one of her favourite topics. 'You don't see many black people in Belfast. I used to love working over by the university because at least you saw all kinds of people over there; people from all over the world. Would you not like to meet different people and learn new languages? There's so much on offer for young people now but you have to get out of Belfast. Wouldn't you like to live somewhere else?'

'Of course. If I get my exams I'll probably go to England to study for a degree.'

'That would be great, love. I'd love to go to a big city with all those different people, all races and colours.'

We small-talked before Mum asked a question that must have been on her mind for years, 'Would you be interested in finding your father, love?'

'No.'

'Why not? Are you not curious? Would you not like to see what he looks like?'

'You're my mum and that's all I need to know. I love you and I have a brilliant family.'

She seemed conflicted by this response, 'Sure think about it. Maybe when you're older.'

'Maybe,' I said but I didn't mean it. Part of me felt a little embarrassed by the whole idea. I wasn't used to the idea of having an African father. I could not have felt more Irish at the time. I had also started reading books about black politics, *The Autobiography of Malcolm X* in particular, and *Soledad Brother* by George Jackson, but these books were about black militancy and 'no sell out' slogans. I was hungry for American notions of blackness, but not for Ghana. Who'd ever heard of Ghana? I could relate to America, I knew nothing about West Africa.

I was amazed by the story that Mum had told me but the bottom line was that she was still my mum and so I found it relatively easy to process. Had she told me that she was not my mum I might have felt uneasy or upset. I might have felt that I did need to find one of my blood parents but this was not the case. I viewed it all positively. I had a warm glow about Mum's love for me, but I had always had that. Despite our tense relationship, I had always known she loved me. I loved Mum's story on a human level, as a family drama, and I was happy to keep it just between us for now. I didn't want new and uncertain aspects of my background to be brought to light. I was happy with my place in the world. I was still me: still black, Irish and republican. And Mum was still my wonderful mum.

Someone approached us to ask what we were talking about. I got up from the seat and as I did, Mum said, 'That's our wee secret, baby.'

'Mum's the word,' I said, laughing.

By the time I went to bed that night, my only concern was getting back to Belfast the next morning in time for the start of the concert. I was tired and my sleep was restful. Not everyone was to be so lucky that night.

From Live Aid to Liverpool

'Has anyone seen Mum?' I asked anxiously as the house began to stir the next morning. No one had seen her. No one knew where she had gone. Chris and I jumped into the car. I suggested that she might have gone for a walk along by the sea, although for Mum, at that time of the morning and after the amount of drink she had consumed, this was a fanciful notion.

With increasing apprehension, we searched the village. Its empty streets added to the ominous sense of gloom. We drove in circles and then decided to try the road to Belfast. Some distance out of the town, we spotted Mum walking along the road. She turned as we drew alongside her. When she recognised the car, she peered through the windscreen, staring hard at us, as if we were the last people in the world she wanted to see. She wanted to be alone and seemed to be struggling to contain her anger. Her lips were moving and her facial expression seemed to convey two contradictory messages: 'What kept you?' and 'What do you want?' I have a vague recollection that she may have said 'No!' as if responding to an order. She was angry, snarling almost.

'What are you doing Mum?' I asked.

'Going home! What does it look like?'

I quickly clambered into the back of the car and she sat in

the front passenger seat. There was very little in the way of conversation. The abruptness of her comments shut down any notion of remarking on the weather, the scenery or the events of the party: 'Turn that radio down! Who was up when you left the house?'

If I asked her anything one-word answers were shot back at me, so I stopped speaking. Mum ordered Chris to stop the car. She got out and, using the open door as cover from other traffic, she crouched down for a toilet break. This was alarming behaviour. For the remainder of the journey, she was quiet. Chris and I breathed a little easier as she drifted off to sleep.

When we got home, I watched Live Aid at quite a low volume. Mum lay under a rug on her favourite, two-seater sofa. I was struggling to work out what was going on. Initially, I put her mood down to a hangover and hoped she would be feeling much better after some decent sleep. But, if some of her mood was alcohol-related, some of it also had to do with her revelations the night before. She must have felt tremendously vulnerable telling a secret that she had kept for nineteen years and her defensiveness was almost certainly an attempt to regain some control over the situation.

What had been one of the more memorable nights of my life had turned into a nervy, tense experience by the following afternoon. The moments of euphoria, poignancy and sadness from the concert in London added to the maelstrom of emotions. Mum's mood was virtually the third person in the room. I jumped to her every demand for more water or headache tablets. Her tone of voice indicated her shifting moods. I only relaxed when she was sleeping.

'Do you want tea and toast?' I asked at regular intervals when she woke up and said nothing, staring at the screen. I tried to break the uncomfortable silence with pleasing small talk and an eagerness to be accommodating, but to no avail. 'Is that still on?' she snapped. Or, more softly, 'What's happening now?' She perked up when Geldof boasted that Ireland was outperforming the English in donations per capita.

Any Anglo-Irish rivalry was always likely to pique her interest. She was awake, too, when David Bowie introduced the devastatingly moving video of famine scenes played to an accompaniment of The Cars' minor-key classic, 'Drive'.

We had our tea with hardly a word. I never raised Mum's revelations from the night before because the atmosphere had changed so markedly. I also felt that there was nothing else to say. It only added to my love for her and made me realise that she had been heroic on my behalf. Chris sat in the kitchen reading a newspaper and watching the portable TV. He couldn't fathom Mum's change either and she was certainly not in the mood to talk about it. She was by turns silent and sorry; angry and aggressive. She came round a bit after we had some dinner. This was the quiet before our own personal storm.

I assumed things would gradually return to normal, which they did, more or less. But it was a fragile, strained version of normality. Commands replaced conversation, or they did for me at least. Mum was in bad form every day, but for other people she put on a show of good humour and laughs. Where possible she tried to avoid meeting anyone outside the family. If she had any visitors or had to attend a family function she complained of being sick of the pressure. She didn't talk about what was wrong and I had long since stopped asking her questions unless they were about practical matters. Raising the issue of what might be on her mind only invited replies such as, 'Never you mind' or, 'Nothing. Nothing's wrong.' I lived day-to-day hoping that she would return to her old self.

We headed off to Majorca again some weeks after Mum had revealed her secret to me. She suggested that I invite my friend Patricia, who worked in the hairdressers with me, to come out to Spain and sneak into our apartment. Ciaran, my eldest brother was also at the same resort with his family, as were my uncle Vivian and his children who stayed in the same apartments as us. Mum was tense. She liked her own space and was a creature of habit. This being so, two weeks spent sharing cramped living quarters with family and friends meant making compromises she didn't have to at home. People were looking to have a good time, Mum wasn't in the mood – something had to give.

Mum's main concern was getting a great tan – an all-over tan. She loved the sun and sunbathed whenever possible. At home, she took advantage of our semi-enclosed back garden to lie for hours on end in various states of undress, including total nudity. Approaching the back of our house on sunny days was best done cautiously, as Mum could often be found lying face down, bra-strap undone and some sort of skirt or bit of material worn in a bespoke way, her legs bare. As we were putting our bags in the car to head to the airport, Mum had warned: 'Now, when you're on the beach, you'll see women sunbathing topless. Don't be staring at them. In fact, just pretend you've seen it all before.' Of course, we had seen it all before – in our own back garden. I thought it best not to point this out.

In Majorca, Mum would sometimes take herself some distance down the beach to be alone, so that she could lie topless. I returned to the apartment in the middle of the afternoon and found the door ajar. When I walked in, Mum was lying on the sun-drenched balcony in a near-naked state. She grabbed a towel and shouted at me, 'Frig you! You scared me, Timothy. Why didn't you knock?'

'Because the door was already open,' I said.

'You better watch your cheek. I'm just about sick of you.'

Such exchanges usually took place in private, so even though Patricia was sharing our apartment, she didn't see or hear much or, like many of my friends, she pretended not to notice when Mum lost her temper within earshot.

Mum could never countenance me arguing back to her, although my brothers did so regularly. While she lost her temper with them, too, they did get to make their point. By now the issue was not what I was saying when I argued with her but rather that I had the 'cheek' to argue at all. Like many mothers, she had an idealised notion of how all of her sons should behave but within our family, she held us to varying standards and she enforced her sanctions with blatantly unequal severity. I seemed to be held accountable more than my brothers.

That night, Patricia wanted to go for a drink. I had little taste for beer and so drank something sweeter. My knowledge of spirits was limited so I opted for Pernod with lots of blackcurrant. When I got back to the apartment I was drunk. Mum slept on one sofa bed in the living room of the apartment and I slept across the room opposite her. With stone floors and bare white walls, every sound in the room was amplified. In the living area, I stumbled around a bit.

'Shut up with your big noise!' Mum hissed through the darkness.

The following morning around 9 a.m. she was first up and this, it went without saying, meant I must get up, too. She asked me where I'd been and what I'd been drinking, as if I was her husband and had just drunk the family housekeeping money. I had the distinct impression that any answer I gave was going to be wrong.

'Pernod.'

'Pernod? I'll Pernod you.'

She moved forward as though she was going to hit me and as I instinctively swayed to avoid her, her fingernail caught my skin at the side of my eye socket. A layer of skin was scraped and hung by a thin sliver from my face. The sun had made me go blacker than ever and my dark skin threw this pinkish-red scar into even sharper relief. I picked off the hanging bit of skin. She looked at me and walked away but, with the rooms taken, there was nowhere for us to go to be away from each other. I sat down on the sofa confused and frustrated.

Mum started to make breakfast and in a normal, almost soft voice, said: 'We've no bread or bottled water.' She rarely apologised to me, explicitly. Once, when I was a boy, she wouldn't let me leave the table until I'd eaten my lunch of scrambled egg. I've never eaten an egg whether boiled, fried, poached or scrambled. I sat at the table picking at tiny morsels as the food went cold. Only when every last child had gone back to school and I was late for my class did she allow me to leave the table. 'Timothy, get ready for school, love,' she shouted in from the living room in a soft voice. I slid off the seat and went to walk out the back door. 'Come on in here a minute,' she said as she sat in the living room having some tea. When I walked in she nodded to some biscuits sitting on the chair beside her, 'Take some of those.' I opened the packet and took two. She gave me a hug and a kiss on the cheek. 'Now run to school and if the teacher asks why you were late tell her you were helping your mammy in the house.' The moment has never left me. Her tone of voice was her way of apologising.

I offered to go to the local Spanish supermarket and she was pleased that I had made the offer. 'Would you, love?' The term of endearment was another peace offering on her part. When I returned with the food, Mum was still the only one up and about. She came over to me with a tube of ointment and applied some to the scrape.

'I'm really sorry, love. I just ...'

'Don't worry about it, Mum,' I said. The world righted itself. My mood changed instantly because she had apologised. She asked what I would say to the others. 'I'll say I scraped it in the bushes outside. Anything. Don't worry.' We spent the rest of the holiday in an uneasy truce.

Back home, a few weeks before starting my A levels, I got a taxi back from a night in town. There was rioting at what we called 'the front of the road', the point where Beechmount meets the Falls Road. I got out of the taxi and walked across a short stretch of no-man's-land between the British Army, RUC jeeps and the rioters.

There was a lull in the rioting and I chatted casually with my pals. I was wearing a suit, with a skinny tie and a tiepin. As I was getting an update from friends about what was going on, I heard the roar of Land Rovers' engines and amid shouts of, 'Here's the fuckin' peelers!' everyone scattered. I ran down the street, knowing that in Northern Ireland guilt by association was a cornerstone of the law. Worse the wear for drink I dived over a low garden wall and tried to hide. Before I knew it I was being bundled into the back of a police jeep. 'Leave him a-fucking-lone, youse Orange bastards!' shouted some of the rioters from the relative safety of the bottom of the street. Closer to my ear and more ominous was the dreaded drone of a smug, sectarian policeman. 'Let me see your hands, you fenian bastard!' he shouted. They were checking to see if my hands were dirty from stone-throwing. They were clean. Even so, I was arrested, charged and found guilty of riotous behaviour. I got fined seventy-five pounds. Mum was outside the court when I got out and was less than impressed by me, despite my pleas that I had been stitched up. As I tried to tell her that I couldn't have been rioting as I had been out, pointing out my style of dress, she said, 'Give over.'

There were only a few weeks to go until I started the College of Business Studies to do my A levels. Those weeks were slowly but surely becoming extremely difficult. Every time I walked in the door Mum was in foul form. Her tone was angry, she would tut audibly and her questions seemed to be provocative. 'Where were you?' or 'What time do you call this?' or 'I suppose you've been running around town?' She constantly asked where I had been, who I had been with and what I had been up to. When I started college in September 1985 things didn't get any better. She would give me the third degree when I got in the door at night. Even when I went shopping for her she seemed to find fault with everything, 'Is that ham fresh? Did you let him give you the ham from the top that the flies have been all over?' She made me return ham or other products to the shop, claiming that they were unsatisfactory. If I had the money I would sometimes pay for replacement ham, meat or bread. I tossed away the stuff Mum considered stale, going off or in some other way below her quality threshold. I found it extremely draining. My friend at college, Billy Bittles, with his mohican hairstyle, eyeliner and bracelets had a much more relaxed family life. He often asked why I didn't just get the items in the corner shop instead of running from Littlewoods to Marks & Spencer and panicking if they didn't have the exact ham or the right kind of loaf. I just told him Mum was very fussy.

Sitting by a roaring fire in our living room one evening towards the end of that summer, I fell asleep. I woke with a jolt as Mum hit my legs.

'Sit up right!' she said, her face the picture of fury.

'What's wrong with you?' I demanded.

'Nothing! Nothing's wrong,' she screamed. 'Don't you ever raise your voice to me!'

She went back into the kitchen and slammed the pots, pans and cupboard doors with all her might. When she came back into the living room I was sitting on the chair she liked to sit on. 'Move,' she said before sitting down with her dinner on a plate on her lap. She told me my dinner was in the kitchen. I lifted it and came into the living room, so I could eat while watching the news. We sometimes sat at our table and sometimes in the living room; there was no particular pattern. As I began to eat, Mum told me to go into the kitchen. As I got up, she said, 'Get out!'

'What?'

'Get out … Just go. I can't have you in my house. Go on, get out.'

As I got up, I glanced at her – she was crying. This alarmed me more than anything. I was used to her anger, but her tears were usually only shed at moments of real despair. I knew that she was profoundly upset but I was weary of her constantly directing her anger at me. As I walked towards the kitchen, she glanced over then looked down at her plate. I left.

I phoned her the next day and in a soft, concerned voice she told me to come home. 'Do you need anything in town?' I asked as a peace offering. 'Yes, love,' she said. I knew that the term of endearment was an olive branch. 'Can you get ham from Littlewoods, four slices of pork shoulder and some mature cheddar? Will you get a plain loaf? Check the date, won't you? Have you got money? Take what I owe you out of my bag when you come home.' And, with that, normal service was resumed. There was no big apology, no hug and no kiss. Instead, and this was often the way with mum, she chose a neutral subject and began to speak about it in an animated fashion. I never ever looked for apologies, I just wanted calm. I said sorry to her but made it clear that I wasn't sure what I did wrong. I took her tone of voice as an acknowledgement that she knew I was not at fault. But I was still worried about her. I thought she might be heading for a breakdown. She was being treated for 'nerves' and eventually developed shingles, probably as a result of stress.

In the meantime I was happy with my low-key Sinn Féin role, selling papers, putting up election posters and doing the collections. Mundane political work it may have been, but it was not without the occasional incident. On Saturday afternoons in the mid-eighties, I used to collect money in a plastic can for Mid-Falls Sinn Féin from three bars, Hines', The Beehive and The Rock Bar. I always left The Rock until the end. All three were working-class bars frequented mainly by men having a drink while placing bets on the racing or the football. I had a plastic collection jar on a string. I made my rounds without menace, collecting loose change. People were free to say no and many did. Usually a shake of the head or an, 'I've no change,' sufficed. Now and again someone would reply with a 'No chance!' and I simply moved on.

'Collection for Sinn Féin?' was my usual line. Men donated coppers and small silver, occasionally a pound coin. On one particular day I was frustrated at missing the TV build-up to the FA Cup Final between Liverpool and Everton. I didn't want to miss the kick off and getting soaked in a sudden shower as I made my way along the Falls Road didn't help my mood. When I made it as far as The Rock the upstairs lounge bar was reasonably busy. I started at the back and soon came to a table where two men, in their mid-to-late twenties, sat drinking. They each had a pint in their hands and a couple of untouched pints sat on the small round table in front of them. One of the two was a large, red-haired man with a seemingly cheery disposition. Or so I thought.

'Sinn Féin?' I said, shaking the tin.

'What to fuck's a nigger like you doing collecting for Sinn Féin?' the cheery guy said, his body undulating as he chuckled away at his joke.

'What did you say?' My response was more of a challenge than a request for clarification.

'I said, "What to fuck's a nigger like you doing collecting for Sinn Féin?"' he repeated, still laughing.

Without saying a word, I lifted a full pint from his table and poured it over his head. He was shocked and instantly stood up.

Still with an empty pint glass in my hand, I backed away from the table. He lifted another full pint and hurled it at head height towards me. I hunkered down and watched it travel through the air almost upright and, with most of its contents still in the glass, smash off the front of the bar. Before I could move, my attacker had gripped me by the throat and hauled me onto my tiptoes. He was shouting at me. I still had the empty pint glass in my hand. I raised it up to the side of his head with my right hand. In a split second, I was pulled back by men who raced over from all corners of the bar. The fat guy was bundled away, too.

'Whoa, easy there lads.'

'What's going on, Tim? What's the problem?'

I then noticed a crowd of IRA men and republican supporters. I walked away towards the door, angry and breathing heavily. Adrenalin surged through me. They insisted that I finish the collection, which I did. As I headed for the exit the fat guy came towards me arms outstretched, willing to shake hands. I accepted. He gestured at his own sodden clothes and laughed: 'Look at the state of me! Can I buy you a pint?' I mumbled my excuses, told him not to worry about it and headed home.

A day or two later, two men called to my house and told me they'd heard about the incident, although neither was in the bar at the time.

'We can have him shot, Tim. Do you want him sorted out?'

'What?' I laughed at the idea.

'You were doing work for the movement,' the elder of the two said.

'Let it go,' I said.

'You sure, Tim?'

'Yeah.'

'OK. But if you ever get hassle like that again, let us know.'

'Will do.'

If I decided to have everyone shot who ever made a racist remark to me there would be a blood bath. They were satisfied once they had made it clear to me that my back was covered. I knew this but it was good to have it reiterated.

During the time I was studying for my A levels, from 1985 to 1987, the Provisional IRA became extremely active, especially in Belfast. Across the north, republicans always looked to Belfast as a barometer of how well the armed struggle was going. On the Falls Road almost all my friends were republican supporters and activists. Many could have gone on to well-paid jobs and good careers but they focused on getting the Brits out. I was more selfish and enjoyed studying and reading for exams in politics, sociology and English literature.

I was very left wing, showing up to class with a Colonel Gaddafi T-shirt on, much to the annoyance of Pat McCann, my English lecturer. He had taught in Libya and told the entire class some harsh truths about life there for ordinary Libyans. The Americans had bombed Gaddafi's residence in 1986, killing a child in the process, and I was happy to show solidarity against Reagan and Thatcher.

Pat's classes and enthusiasm brought books like *King Lear* and *Dr Faustus* to life for me and made me eager to learn. If I passed my exams a place studying politics at Liverpool Polytechnic was mine for the taking. I chose it, Manchester and a few other northern English towns over colleges further south but I knew that I didn't want to study in Belfast. No one was more in favour of people living the full college experience than Mum. She wanted me to go to London – 'It's big and exciting,' she said. 'Why stay in this place, sure you know it inside out? In London, you'll meet people from all over the world.' But she was happy with Liverpool because she knew I had chosen it for similar reasons. I wanted to live in a culturally diverse city with a large black population, just to see if and how it was different to Belfast. As it transpired, my first year was spent on the edge of the city close to a particularly white and very working-class estate called Huyton. The high walls of the campus grounds physically and psychologically segregated us from the 'scallies', as we sometimes referred to the scousers. They saw us as 'yuppies' and 'snobs', which may have been true for some but certainly not all of us. There were some black students around but most were not on my course. I tended to mix with people on the social studies course and my closest friends were white, except for an Indian girl called Sangita who became something of a soul mate.

There were nine accommodation blocks on the sprawling campus, some about ten storeys high, the rest more compact. I was lumped in a block which housed most of the Irish students – they'd put us altogether as this meant we had something in common. I was not overjoyed at having left Ireland to meet a more ethnically diverse group of people, only to find myself in a block with students from Newry and Tyrone. At times, though, such as when Ireland beat England 1–0 in the European Championships in Germany in 1988, we had a great time flying flags and giving the English students lots of friendly abuse. I was surprised to see how much this meant to me, but then 1988 was a difficult year to be away from home.

Instead of meeting black people and becoming more aware of black culture, I actually became very patriotic and emphasised my Irish identity. This was, in part, due to the constant news from home. The SAS shot dead three IRA volunteers in Gibraltar in March 1988. I knew one of them, Mairead Farrell. The incident set in motion a deadly sequence of events. When the bodies of the IRA volunteers were brought back from Gibraltar a loyalist, Michael Stone, attacked their funeral in Milltown Cemetery with guns and grenades, killing three more people including IRA volunteer Kevin Brady. Three days later at Brady's funeral, two British soldiers drove into the midst of the cortege in west Belfast. The mourners thought this was another loyalist attack, especially when one of the occupants of the car produced a weapon. Surrounded by thousands of angry republicans including members of the IRA, the soldiers had driven their car in various directions in an attempt to escape, before finally reaching a dead end. They were beaten in the most horrendous circumstances by scores of mourners and then shot dead by the IRA.

During this period I was watching on my little portable TV in my student digs. It all seemed surreal. I felt guilty about heading out to clubs and sitting around talking about European political systems when people were dying back home. I applied for a transfer to Queen's University in Belfast and was accepted. I had decided to do the remaining two years of my degree at home. After some weeks of deliberation, I realised that the people of west Belfast were hardly waiting for me to come back to save them. I decided to stay in Liverpool. And besides, I was enjoying the student life, the football and the lively social life.

The turmoil at home meant that on St Patrick's Day it was important for me to display my Irish roots, so that year I wore a shamrock and a Celtic top that a girl I had been seeing in Belfast had bought me – even though I have never really supported the team beyond hoping they would beat Rangers.

When I came home for a holiday I was in the passenger seat of my friend's taxi. We drove into an RUC checkpoint. The cops recognised me and ordered us out of the taxi. I had the Celtic jersey in a bag. During the search one cop found it.

'Celtic? You are a star, Brannigan. You really are a star,' he repeated sarcastically.

The cops would always express surprise – and then contempt – for my involvement in and support for republicanism. One Sunday afternoon I decided to go up to Milltown Cemetery to see the IRA and republican plots. Near the gates, two RUC Land Rovers pulled over and some cops jumped out. Petty harassment helped them pass the day. A pretty, female cop spoke. After the usual name and address routine, she asked a simple but surprising question, 'Why are you a republican?'

She waited on my answer, 'You not talking, Tim?' Standing off to one side, she looked me up and down. 'What are you doing? You're a good-looking guy. Do you really want to be associated with the IRA? With murderers?' She stared at me. 'Nothing to say for yourself?' They noted the time and details, my response and the fact that I was alone, got back into the jeeps and drove off. I was pleased with the unexpected compliment and had been tempted to come back with some smart or flirty one-liner but the humourless-looking grunt standing alongside her had glared at me hard enough to suggest that if I tried to be clever I'd end up in the back of the jeep.

Giving the RUC cheeky responses did sometimes provoke reactions. I was once out cycling on a racing bike when I got chased through streets near my home. Eventually they caught up with me and asked a long series of questions, many of which I refused to answer. A moustachioed peeler began to lose his temper. He took my silence to be insolence. 'What's the matter? Don't you understand the Queen's English?' he demanded.

'I'm well aware that the Queen is English,' I replied.

'Right, that's it. You're under arrest. Take off your socks and shoes,' he said.

'What for?'

'We believe you're equipped to go joyriding. Take your shoes off.'

'Well, not only do I not steal cars, but I can't drive.'

'Take your shoes off!' They grabbed me and began to pull my shoes off. One cop tried to grab my bike as others threw me into the jeep. People shouted abuse at them and words of support to me. I was taken to Springfield Road barracks where one cop said, 'Throw him in a cell to cool off!' Like I was the one who'd lost my temper.

They stood shouting abuse and laughing outside my cell. After a silence and some whispering they then sang the chorus of a popular song from the era: 'Free Nelson Mandela. Free, free, free Nelson Mandela.' They released me, without charge, a few hours later.

I was used to such treatment and while it was interesting that the RUC and the Brits had an opinion on me at all, I would rather have been able to blend into the background.

Back in England I was learning that Liverpool was hardly an enlightened haven of multi-cultural awareness either. As much as I loved it, it was a harsh, hard city. Thatcher had it in for its citizens and some of their local politicians were on ego trips. Low-level racial tension seemed to simmer just below the surface as the two communities left each other to their own devices. Liverpool's long-established black community lived mainly to the south of the city centre in the Toxteth/Liverpool 8 area. The housing was shocking, worse than most of the housing in working-class Belfast, and unemployment levels were very high. Many of the shops were derelict. Students frequented the area for late-night counter-culture bars and the thrill of saying they had been hanging out in Toxteth, which had an edgy reputation because of the 1981 riots. I rarely went there because my friends were happier to hang out in the student union and the usual student-friendly bars and none of us knew anyone from Toxteth.

In the city centre, black faces were almost as scarce as they were in Belfast, despite the fact that in Liverpool there are thousands of black people. Politicians and commentators in Liverpool, so far as I could make out, claimed that the black people 'kept themselves to themselves'. Local white people said that, too, as if this segregation was self-imposed and self-perpetuating. The blacks, in response, said that they were victims of discrimination and this 'debate' went round in circles for years.

In my second and third years I lived about half a mile from Toxteth but I may as well have been on a different planet – most students didn't mix with the local black community, or indeed with the general Liverpool population. In most of the bars that I drank in, there were few black people and those who did socialise in these establishments were often, like me, black people from places other than Liverpool. We sometimes went to a club that attracted a lot of black scousers. It was very edgy and we had a vague sense that there could be trouble as a 'them and us' atmosphere seemed to develop. My friends were all white, so, naturally, felt a little apprehensive but there was never any trouble.

I loved Liverpool but not the distance away from Belfast during what proved to be a momentous period of the Troubles, with Beechmount often at the centre of IRA activity. My dissertation for my course, *Whose Finger is on the Trigger?*, was on the causes of the Troubles and was dedicated to the memory of Eamon Quinn, a friend of my brother's who was shot dead by loyalists. These were dangerous times for everyone. I would never have guessed but people were making decisions that would lead to a sea of troubles arriving at our door.

The IRA Comes Calling

In July 1990 I had the world exactly where I wanted it. I had just graduated with a degree and the prospect of a new job in a new city, or possibly even a new country, was tantalisingly close. But I didn't get a job right away. I moved to London and then Surrey but by September I had run out of money. Deflated, I went back home for proper meals and a break.

Belfast felt safe and familiar. I envisaged a few weeks recharging my batteries before heading back to England. I had been burned out by my finals and by the struggle to find a decent job or even a decent casual job to see me through. I wanted to be in London. These were the thoughts in my head that autumn in Mum's house in Belfast. And then, while I was home alone, there was a knock at the door.

There is no special sign or signal when the IRA comes calling. There are no elaborate procedures, no masks, no guns and no talk about having to do your duty for Ireland. It's not like the terrible TV dramas and movies. Instead, when they come, they rely on past encounters, family connections, friendships and the general ethos of anti-Britishness. It's not necessarily a hatred of all things British. I certainly didn't hate British people or British culture. I just didn't think their army should be in our country. And, given my experiences at their hands, I still feel that I had every right to oppose their presence. And so when the IRA did come calling my impulse was to help them. Although, initially I didn't feel I could.

I knew the two men were in the IRA. I also knew them on a social level but was not a particularly close friend of either. I liked them both, I guess, and one belonged to a family with whom our own family got on well. 'Tell you what it is, Tim – we're stuck,' said the older, taller man. 'We were wondering if we could use your house to leave some stuff. Just a bit o' gear.'

'What is it?' I asked.

'Two chocolate trifles.' That was their rhyming slang for two rifles. 'Any chance?' he continued.

'It's not my house. It's my mum's and she's at work. I couldn't let you use it, lads,' I replied.

'We're really stuck Tim,' he repeated. 'We need to clear a dump because other stuff is coming in. It's only overnight, it'll definitely be away first thing in the morning.'

I felt bad that I couldn't help them and in a situation like this a certain amount of machismo comes into play. I didn't want to let them down.

'Sorry lads, I can't do it. This isn't my house and my ma isn't in.'

'Just till the morning.'

I sighed heavily, 'Look, you can't bring stuff in but if it's only overnight you could dump it in that old car at the side of the house. It's not secure, the doors don't lock, but if anything was quietly left in it overnight, I would never need to know about it.'

They looked up the driveway at the Alfa Romeo and said that they would use it.

It all seemed clean and easy. I didn't have to see or touch the gear and if I said nothing it would be away by morning and no one would be any the wiser. There was no pressure, no threat. It was just a simple request for a favour and, on my part, a slightly reluctant agreement to help. The world seemed very dangerous all of a sudden. I paced the living room and wished it was morning so the weapons would be taken away. I thought about the dangers but reassured myself that nothing could possibly go wrong. I resolved to say nothing to anyone as they headed off to get the rifles.

It was teatime and about thirty minutes later I heard the boot of the car being slammed closed. I didn't see the men or what they had left. I watched the news with a slight sense of unease. Paddy called and asked if I wanted to watch some football in a nearby bar. He also asked me to go with him over to Queen's University to pick Mum up from work in a restaurant there. She finished at 9 p.m. We got into his car and drove down the street. Everything seemed normal. We stopped at the corner shop and as we went in a young guy from our street passed us close to the shop doorway. I didn't even notice him but my brother spotted his nervous, erratic movement. We left the shop after buying chewing gum and then headed on to a bar.

As fate would have it, my brother's car broke down close to Mum's work. We called Ciaran and he drove over and picked us all up and took us back to Mum's house, less than five minutes' drive away. I said nothing about the events of earlier that evening. As we turned the corner into the bottom of our street, my heart leapt into my mouth as scores of cops and Brits were running around. Lights flashed blue on the top of the RUC jeeps. Mum, oblivious of the potential danger, thought it all quite exciting.

'Something must have happened … Wonder what it was?' she said.

'No idea,' I said.

My mind was racing, I was gripped by fear. The cops told us that to get to our house, halfway up the street, we'd have to get out of the car and walk up. Only Mum and I got out of the car. My brothers returned to their own homes. In a split second I resolved not to disappear as it would mean going on the run and, worse, it would have left Mum alone.

As we walked up the street, we noticed that the cops were searching every house on our side of the street, up to and including our own. Voices were raised and children shouted noisily. People speculated over garden hedges.

'It's bloody ridiculous, so it is,' said one woman.

'What's going on?' Mum shouted to neighbours.

'We don't know Peggy but they're raiding everybody's houses.'

Mum seemed cheery; I tried to keep my composure. Because not much time had passed, I was fairly sure the gear was still in the car, but I was thrown by the fact that so many houses had been searched. Perhaps the IRA had called back while I was out and tried to move the gear to a safer location. Maybe, while doing this, they had been intercepted, I thought. I was anxious but part of me was sure that there must have been developments while I'd been out. I prepared to play dumb.

When we got to our house, the front door had been sledge hammered open. The house was full of cops. I knew I was in trouble by their aggressive demeanour. Grim faces, intense staring and the fact that they had not apologised for their presence or the damage matched the aggression they had shown to gain entry. I knew they suspected something. Mum sat on her favourite chair and I sat on the sofa watching the match, although I was so nervous I couldn't concentrate, while about ten RUC men ransacked the house. An RUC man was assigned to watch us and he tried to stare me out despite the fact that I had my back to him as I watched the football on TV.

'Why are you staring at him?' Mum snapped.

'I have to watch you both. Just doing what I'm told,' he replied.

I prayed silently. From the many raids in the 1970s I knew that we had the right to accompany them around our house in case they wrecked anything. I had good reason to worry; it later transpired that they had found my set of professionally-taken graduation photos and had written 'UVF' across my forehead and, 'You fucking dickhead spick bastard' across the main photograph.

Without asking permission, I went upstairs to my own bedroom, only to be confronted by a cop who was bent over, his head buried deep in my wardrobe.

'Be careful in there,' I said in a poor effort at sounding unfazed.

He stopped ransacking my clothes when he heard my voice. 'Why?' he asked, aggressively.

'There's some good gear in there,' I said cheekily.

He was not amused. He grabbed me by the throat and in one movement, pinned me against the bedroom door and hissed, 'See you, you fenian bastard, I'm personally going to shoot you.' This was one of a number of death threats made to me by police officers which they failed to carry out.

Eventually, though, they started to indicate they were about to pack up. I was surprised. I suspected a ruse because they were so aggressive, like they *knew*. They often found the stuff quite quickly but said nothing and, instead, watched home-owners closely to see if body language or a reckless comment suggested prior knowledge. Even as the cops backed out the front door, they kept staring at me. Mum was shouting about wanting her door fixed. I couldn't believe my luck and told her not to worry, that it would all be sorted out. Just as I was about to close the front door, one cop shouted, 'We've found something!'

A senior cop pushed the door back and ordered us back into the living room. I needed to use the toilet but we weren't allowed to move. 'Do not let them near the toilet. Don't let them wash their hands,' the senior cop told the others. I knew I was going to be arrested. I wanted to tell Mum not to worry and to ask her to get me a solicitor when the police took me away but I couldn't get near her to whisper. I should have realised that it would have been perfectly normal to speak to Mum about solicitors given the situation. I assumed that I would be taken away but I didn't expect what happened next. The senior policeman walked into the room. 'Mrs Brannigan, I'm arresting you on suspicion of having possession of guns and explosives with intent to endanger life.'

'Me? Get away,' Mum laughed, scarcely believing her ears.

A policewoman entered the room with clear plastic bags

and told Mum she was going to put them on her hands. 'What explosives?' I thought. I also wondered why on earth they were arresting Mum. I certainly hadn't reckoned on that. Mum pleaded with them to allow her to change out of her work uniform, a pinafore. 'I'll just run upstairs and get something, I can't go out dressed like this,' she said, tugging at her uniform.

'You'll be fine the way you are, Mrs Brannigan,' the policewoman said.

'Well, can I brush my hair?' Mum asked.

They formally told me that I was also being arrested, as was Chris who had, himself, just arrived home from work. Plastic bags were placed on my hands and I was handcuffed and taken out of our house, and placed in a Land Rover to be taken to Castlereagh Interrogation Centre. Mum was placed in another jeep that would follow behind. My heart was in my mouth. I told a fresh-faced, obviously new, cop that I needed the toilet. He informed a much older cop standing nearby, whom I recognised as the one who threatened me in my bedroom an hour earlier. He stared at me for several seconds and then said: 'Fuck him!'

I wondered what Mum was thinking. The one thing I hadn't bargained on in discussions with republican-minded friends about Castlereagh over the years was that my mum would be there with me. That altered the situation emphatically, as it meant I had to worry about someone other myself. Worse still, Mum was innocent and I felt responsible for her. There were other shocks to come for us both.

Castlereagh

'Fuck! I thought they were joking when they said we'd got a nigger,' a grinning CID detective sneered, entering the room where I was being fingerprinted and swabbed. This might be a long few days, I thought. As I was being processed, various cops, in and out of uniform, came to gawk, smirk or make some joke. I blanked them out and was more concerned about my mug shot. I was determined to smile or even grin, simply because they insisted that we should not do so. As it turned out, I looked stunned at the moment a Polaroid camera captured for posterity the start of one of the biggest tests life could possibly throw my way.

The IRA was the obvious target for my anger. I wondered if some IRA people had been arrested, too, I just didn't know. How on earth had such a simple operation gone wrong so quickly? If IRA men were caught with me then fair enough, but all I could think about was that my family were facing jail. During those first couple of hours I found it easier to blame the IRA than myself but it soon passed.

The processing dragged on. A forensics expert scraped samples of dirt from under my fingernails and swabbed me for explosives traces. I prayed that Mum would not try and take the blame for me. I was worried that she would prioritise my freedom above her own and an uncomfortable thought gnawed away at the back of my head; perhaps I should do whatever it took to rescue her.

The RUC would attempt to disorient us. All belongings – watches, belts and jewellery – would be removed and if a person was caught at or near an incident or was suspected of having handled weapons or explosives they would often be stripped and placed in deliberately ill-fitting, navy boiler suits. The sleeves could be too long or too short and this permanent sense of discomfort was designed to help break down republicans. Mum, Chris and I were given boiler suits and canvas deck shoes, without laces of course, to wear. My awareness of the RUC's methods meant their psychological edge was blunted. I had been informed of many of the techniques used by the police and was intrigued as they were introduced throughout the process. Mum and Chris, however, had no such knowledge.

Castlereagh is an unremarkable 1960s brown brick building, a few storeys high, surrounded by the normal security paraphernalia: high fences, bulletproof glass, cameras, lookout posts and men with guns. Situated in east Belfast, it became synonymous with severe beatings, psychological torture and 'inhuman treatment' in the late 1970s, according to a report by the European Court of Human Rights. I had spoken many times formally and informally with other republicans about how people we knew had either 'broken' – made incriminating statements – in Castlereagh or had remained silent and 'walked'. Without doubt, many IRA volunteers were questioned about shootings and attacks that they had, indeed, carried out. Without witnesses and corroborating evidence, remaining silent meant the RUC had no evidence. I hadn't seen or touched the weapons and there could be no physical evidence that I had been involved in their transport or maintenance. I knew that I had a great chance of walking – if I stayed silent.

Interrogations – they called them interviews – took place in claustrophobic rooms with humming fluorescent lights and no windows. The heat was oppressive. There was a basic office desk and two chairs next to each other for the cops. A solitary chair sat on the other side of the desk. There was a video camera up on the wall in the corner, placed there for the protection of prisoners. The cops laughed and told me it didn't work.

RUC interrogators attempt to appear omniscient. Their information comes from surveillance equipment, touts, undercover soldiers, the SAS, MI5, CID, guesswork, tip-offs from the public and informers. The detectives would casually mention IRA volunteers by name or even nickname, watching closely to see if I gave a flicker of reaction. Informers, or touts as we preferred to call them, were valuable to Special Branch, giving regular, often daily updates not just on weapons and explosives, imminent attacks and IRA activity but also on the private lives of volunteers. The RUC compiled endless trivia on republicans: where they drank; where they slept (many republicans slept in safe houses and sometimes in a series of them for fear of assassination); who was having an affair; who had a drink problem. This information could then be mentioned in Castlereagh making the republican feel that his whole lifestyle had been spied on. Sometimes the cops did know the entire story, sometimes they had part of the picture, and sometimes they were bluffing. However, neither they nor we republicans ever had perfect knowledge of the situation. That the IRA got away and only Mum, Chris and I were arrested must have made for a very poor second prize. A possible conviction, for sure, but the IRA people involved with the weapons were major players.

The cops could hold us for up to seven days and then they would have to charge or release us. My captors didn't all possess first-class detective minds. Some may well have, but mostly they were simply working to a formula. They did so for a reason, though; it brought results. I knew not to under-estimate them. Pádraic Wilson, a Belfast republican I knew from the 1980s, had come to a Sinn Féin meeting to speak to us at length about his experiences in Castlereagh and his descriptions of CID tactics were to prove extremely accurate, enabling me to keep some measure of control in the battle for psychological superiority.

Interrogations began at 9 a.m. and lasted until around lunchtime. We got an hour's break and then there were more interviews from 2 p.m. to 5 p.m., then tea until around six in the evening. A final session took place in the evening and could last until close to midnight. The detectives worked in relays, trying different approaches and personalities but they were all variations on good cop, bad cop. I had four interrogators working in pairs. I gave the main couple nicknames. One, a pale, grey-haired, skinny man, I called John Inman because he looked a little like the star of the 1970s' TV show *Are You Being Served?* He generally played good cop. I decided to call the bad cop Darth Vader, after he taunted me about invading my personal space: 'Do you know what this is?' he asked, drawing an imaginary bubble around me with an arcing sweep of his index finger. He didn't bother waiting on the answer I wasn't about to give.

'That's your personal space. You don't like me invading it. I make you feel uncomfortable, don't I? If we were in a bar you wouldn't mind because different rules apply there. But this?' he edged closer. 'You don't like me in your personal space one bit, do you, Brannigan?' He was right, I didn't like it but I was momentarily preoccupied with the notion of someone invading my space. My own personal space-invader. Aliens ... space ... Darth Vader! The moniker suited him. He behaved a bit like an excitable schoolboy and bragged that he would shoot dead any IRA men who dared try to kill him.

I prepared myself mentally for several days of saying nothing. It remains the best defence against any police questioning. For the first session I walked in and, quite deliberately, moved the chair away from the centre of the desk off to one side so that I, not they, decided where I sat. The detectives were business-like in their suits, bad ties and aftershave. I was trying to work out which pose on my chair looked the most casual, the most 'Who gives a fuck?'. Suspecting that none of my attitude had registered, I then rocked back on my chair, with my feet off the floor and my shoulder blades leaning against the wall for balance. Darth Vader roared, 'Sit up straight!' I did, then waited about twenty seconds before slowly forcing my body weight against the back of the chair so I was back on the two hind legs of the chair again. We were to repeat this little war of attrition throughout the day.

They asked the same question in one hundred different ways and spoke about the 'moral shame' of republican actions, the innocent people that the IRA had killed and how, morally, I was 'just as guilty' as any gunman. I folded my arms and looked bored. It was this psychological pressure that undid many activists, although beatings were also a key weapon in the RUC's arsenal. They offered me menacing reassurance, 'We're not going to beat you. We've got you red-handed so we wouldn't want to jeopardise our case by touching you or leaving any marks.'

I knew that their claims that I was caught 'red-handed' were bullshit. I hadn't touched or even seen the weapons so there was no fingerprint evidence, no fibres from my clothes on the guns and no gun residue on me. The car in our driveway was accessible to anyone. If I said nothing the evidence was, at best, circumstantial. I just had to resist the pressure and keep my nerve. That was easier said than done, as they were threatening to put myself, Mum, Chris and other members of my family in jail. 'We'll just keep arresting people if you don't start talking,' they said.

I was eventually, after many requests, allowed to see my solicitor. He told me that there was a distinct possibility I could 'walk' at any trial and perhaps even get out on bail before too long. It was good to hear something positive. However, events were to unfold that meant his advice became virtually impossible to heed.

The detectives broke up their questions with jokes, speculation and curious, mundane details in an attempt to make me feel anxious about my imminent imprisonment. They said I would be raped in jail because I was 'fresh meat'. John Inman, wearing a shirt that was too big for him, boasted that he would go home after questioning me to 'poke the wife'. I felt like sending her a sympathy card.

At other times, he kept up his humane approach. 'Do you know something, Tim?' he said. 'D'ya see if it wasn't for the violence, I'd probably support a united Ireland. With Europe and all that, it's bound to happen sometime. It's a good cause, a noble cause, but violence, Tim? Violence? You're disgracing your cause by killing people. You must see that ...'

'Oh, for fuck's sake!' I thought. This was the Castlereagh equivalent of the dreaded: 'It's not you, it's me.'

His partner in crime investigations, Darth Vader, liked to ramp up the pressure. He quite deliberately came around to my side of the desk, his mouth and nose close to my ear. I sat, arms folded, looking impassive, although I would sometimes look directly at him to show that I could. At other moments, I would look elsewhere around the room trying to seem casually distracted, uninterested. I yawned. 'Oh! Are we fucking boring you, big lad?' Darth Vader roared in an attempt to intimidate me. 'Well, you may get used to it son, because we've got a lot of questions to ask you and if we don't like the answers we get, you're going to jail.' I responded by picking imaginary bits of fluff off my boiler suit. 'I'd love to punch that black fucking jaw of yours!' said Inman. His good cop masked slipped occasionally. In a fight with him, I'd have fancied my chances even though, ordinarily, I couldn't beat snow off a rope.

Between interrogation sessions I was taken back to my holding cell. These cells were bleak with a light that stayed on day and night, a single bed, a hard, rubber mattress and a smelly, heavily stained blanket. It was stained with blood, sweat and tears: the blood of the beaten, the sweat of the guilty and I suspect, the tears of those for whom long-term imprisonment beckoned. They may have been tears too for those who betrayed their comrades. But I didn't cry, I hadn't betrayed anyone.

When Darth Vader and John Inman were going full pelt I stalled them with requests for tea and regular toilet breaks. They tried to undermine my commitment to the armed struggle, the IRA and the idea of a united Ireland. 'Walking up and shooting an unarmed man in the back of the head?' John Inman said incredulously. 'How could you live with yourself? Do you think that's brave? Do you think that will get you a united Ireland?' I said nothing.

Then they revealed that they had found a copy of my dissertation at my home. They realised that I knew about the politics of Northern Ireland and began to play to my vanity and intellectual pride, admitting that they didn't expect me to fall for their attempts to break me emotionally with talk about 'innocent civilians' dying. I tried to disguise my increasing anxiety about my family with studied nonchalance. I would inspect my nails and pull pensive faces as though the biggest issue in my life at that precise moment was the state of my cuticles.

The primary focus of my interrogators was on demanding names. A secondary line of questioning seemed to be whether I was in the IRA or not. 'What were the names?' Inman asked with a weary sigh. 'Why are you protecting these men? They don't give a fuck about you, Tim. They're very possibly sitting in a bar right now, saying, "Poor Tim – ah, well", and yet you're protecting *them*. Do you think they would protect you? Fucking sure they wouldn't!' he shouted. 'Fucking sure they wouldn't, Tim.' I laughed to myself at this point, because I thought that might be a reasonably accurate summation of the situation. I'm not sure what else, realistically, the IRA were supposed to do. 'Look after number one, Tim,' John Inman advised.

For the first two days I sat silent, although under severe stress I knew that, like me, Mum was in an interrogation room not far away being questioned by people she hated. I prayed that they would let Mum and Chris go and focus on me. They hadn't let me wash and I stank of sweat. Many republicans deliberately didn't wash as the smell made the cops less likely to sit too close and the interview room would be uncomfortable for them too. Some republicans would even piss on their hands and then run their wet hands through their hair for the same reason. There are many stories about how men coped. A man from west Belfast that I would later get to know lay on the floor for the entire seven days. The detectives pulled their chairs over beside him and questioned him for days as he lay there silent, defiant. Another man was refused access to the toilet so he urinated in the corner of the interrogation room in front of them. They let him use the toilet whenever he asked after that.

With a hammer blow I found out that Mum was talking. 'So, you're a bastard, then?' Darth Vader gloated. 'You really are a bastard! Your ma is in there telling us all about you and your father and how he ran off on you. Is that why you want to help the IRA? Are you angry? Do you want to fit in?' An inveterate talker all her life, Mum was discussing intimate family matters with the detectives. Their pretence at concern had fooled her. I was devastated. John Inman spoke in a low, confidential voice: 'Tim, let's sort this out. We don't need to hear all of this ... personal stuff. Just tell us what happened, who called to your house and we can get your mother out of here.'

The sessions blended into one another, and anxiety shredded my insides while the pressure sometimes made my head feel like it would explode. I made regular requests for toilet breaks just so I could think for a second. They went back to asking about the IRA men and the night I was caught. Again and again they tried to piece together my movements that night and they would tell me in detail what I had done: 'So, you were in the house. They left the gear. Your brother brought you to watch football. You stopped at the sweet shop and saw Martin Clarke. You left the shop and drove off ...'

During the second day of questioning I noticed that a crucial detail, which they had been repeating from the start, had disappeared. They had suddenly stopped mentioning Clarke's name and began to emphasise the power of their surveillance techniques. 'You've no idea who we have hiding in the old transit van at the bottom of the street. We have men watching everything.'

By the end of the second day they were bored. One of them, pointing at a brown cardboard folder, said with a little laugh, 'This is your security file.' Darth Vader said he could read the first two lines of my file to me. I was intrigued. He glanced up from the lines he was about to read to make sure he had my attention. 'The first sentence says, "This man is a republican", and the second sentence says, "This man is black".' Clearly, they'd had their top men on the job.

But the lighter moments were few and far between. They talked about the fact that the AK47 that they'd found in the car had been used in fifteen attacks on members of the British Army and the RUC around Beechmount in the previous year or two. John Inman outlined one of my many dilemmas: 'You have been caught with an IRA Active Service Unit's arms dump, Brannigan. You are fucked. *Fucked!* And do you know why you're fucked?' Now, at this stage I could quite possibly have answered his question with a fair degree of accuracy but I got the feeling he was about to tell me anyway. 'You're not fucked because of the AK. You're not fucked because of the other weapons or even the grenades. You're fucked because of the mercury tilts. Those things aren't made for defensive purposes. You can't claim you had them to "defend the area". No chance. That defence is gone, son. Mercury tilts are used for one thing and one thing only – to kill. And do you know who the IRA tries to kill with them? Judges! And judges hate them. Anyone caught with them gets fucking hammered. You're looking at fifteen years, big lad.'

'Maybe more,' Darth Vader chipped in, like he'd brought all of his legal training to bear on the issue, before delivering his considered opinion. In response, I made a point of obviously checking, yet again, the state of my nails.

After forty-eight hours, more devastating news. I learned that, rather than releasing my mum and concentrating on me, they had decided to get an Extension Order for both her and Chris. They were also looking to arrest my brothers, they said. I was in turmoil. Where would it all end? How many of us were going to end up in jail? What should I do? Mum could end up being charged. I knew I could do the seven days but my family weren't prepared, weren't involved in the events that night and hadn't given their consent, yet they were all liable to be arrested. It began to seem as though making a statement accepting total responsibility was my only option, even if it meant certain jail for me – and for some years. I worried that by making a statement I had no guarantee that they would let my family go. It would be one hell of a gamble. I wanted to get them all out but I didn't want people to think I had 'broken like a plate' or signed a statement. I didn't want the stain of being a tout. In Ireland it remains an unforgivable sin. But the prospect of Mum doing another few days was too much to bear. They told me that I could be the 'hard man' if I wanted but that they were thinking of charging Mum, as it was her car and her property. 'How would you like that?' they asked. Doubt started to creep in and I certainly didn't feel like I could gamble with Mum's freedom or future.

Knowing that I was, effectively, signing years of my life away, I made a statement claming that I alone was responsible for the weapons being in the car and that no one else from my family was involved. The statement was relatively short and I composed it in full view of two detectives. I made notes on my hand with the pen and with each sentence I would try and work out what follow-up questions they might ask me afterwards. It took nearly half an hour to write the lines and with that, any hope of Mum, Chris and me going home together died. I was relieved that I had probably done enough for them to ease up on my family. On the other hand, instead of going back to England to join my mates and make a career, I was going to jail for some considerable time.

On that Friday evening, I was sitting in the interrogation room with the detectives questioning me about my statement.

In particular, they now wanted the names of the IRA men who had called to my house. The door behind me opened suddenly and both of my interrogators stood up, lightning fast. 'Sir,' one of them said while running his hand down his tie, checking it was centred. I didn't look around but the two regular detectives left the room with their files under their arm.

A high-ranking detective entered. I knew him by reputation as someone who had survived an IRA attack despite having been shot a number of times. He occasionally appeared on TV and I had heard that the year before I was arrested he was involved in questioning an IRA volunteer from my area who had made a series of detailed statements about some high-profile IRA attacks. Homes in our area were searched based on these statements. The volunteer in question was an unassuming, smiling, likeable guy with impressive reserves of personal bravery. However, I felt let down that he had folded and didn't want to capitulate in a similar fashion.

The senior detective took one of the empty chairs from the desk and placed it beside my chair before sitting down. He stared at the side of my head. I wanted to turn and look at him but I was unsure what was going to happen next so I didn't move. 'Do you know who I am?' he asked. I said nothing. He introduced himself and, bizarrely, handed me his warrant card. I studied it. He acted like he knew I was well aware of who he was. I didn't blink. I didn't want to register any emotion whatsoever. 'I just want to ask you a few questions and you are going to give me some answers,' he said in a tone that suggested he would get what he came for. He produced a little notebook. 'This will be between us. No formal notes. I want to know when you joined the organisation and who recruited you.' I was surprised. The other detectives had asked me the same question with little in the way of conviction. He never used the term 'IRA'. I said nothing.

'Are you a member of the organisation? Who recruited you and when? What was your role?' His tone was deliberate but carried with it the unmistakable suggestion that I was wasting his time and that he would get the information he came for. He again assured me that this discussion was 'off the record'. I thought he was about to try and recruit me as an informer. 'If you think you have a tout on your hands, you are very much mistaken,' I said, confident that I would rather take fifteen years than 'turn' in Castlereagh.

He repeated his questions slowly and deliberately and asked for the names of the IRA men who had called at my door. 'How long have you been in ...' he paused, '... the organisation? What is your role?' He had the cold, dead eyes of a shark and his thin lips and skin suggested a walk in the autumn air might do him the world of good. I didn't speak. There were periods of extended silence as he stared at me and at his notebook. I decided to make a point. 'You know better than me what happened, otherwise I wouldn't be sitting here now,' I said, speculatively. 'Not much happens in west Belfast that I don't know about,' he replied.

He stayed about twenty minutes but at one point he said with certainty that he did not want me as an informer and that I would be 'going to jail'. I said nothing. He got up without a word and left. The other detectives came back in and asked excitedly what had been said and then more aggressively what I knew about the IRA and what had I really been doing in England for the rest of the night. I later found out that they had even got the Anti-Terrorist Squad to raid some of the addresses I had lived at in England.

On the Saturday, they eventually decided to let Mum and I meet for a quick chat. I didn't request it, though she may have. I leaned over and hugged Mum. This was the meeting I both wanted and dreaded. Here, yet again, were Mum's dreams turning to dust. The one son she had tried so hard to protect, whom she had encouraged and pushed towards a university education, the boy she had rescued from instit-utional care was now facing prison and there was nothing she could do to stop it. I wanted to be brave but it was all I could do not to break down. An RUC man, arms folded and emotionless, stood in the room with us, making it difficult to talk openly. He listened to every word we said, but his presence did make things easier in one respect; it stopped me getting too emotional. It was a grey Saturday evening and through a small window, for the first time, I could see daylight. Mum and I embraced and I began to speak softly so the cop couldn't hear but firmly enough so that Mum wouldn't worry about me. 'I'm sorry about all of this, Mum. I'll explain it all but not now. You have to be brave and you have to stop talking about family stuff as they are using what you tell them against me.' We hugged a bit more and we were both composed. 'Mum, I'm very sorry but I am going to be going to jail.'

'I know, love,' she said sympathetically.

She told me to be brave and not get upset. Our foreheads were touching; her hands were on my face. We hugged for a while without saying much and then we kept repeating, 'I love you' but the more intensely we said it, the more I could feel myself filling up. Again, I reminded her not to cry and not to speak to them any more about intimate family details. I wanted to tell her not to speak to them at all, but asking her to adopt an attitude of total silence was unrealistic.

We sat up and she talked more loudly, for the benefit of the cop. With each sentence she winked at me to indicate that we were getting one over on them. Humour comes at the most unlikely times. Mum laughed at one point and told me how one detective was quite fat and, as he interrogated her, all she could see were his shirt buttons straining under the pressure of his massive gut. Mum was repulsed.

He had been playing bad cop while a female detective played good cop. He whipped himself up into a storm of moral outrage, demanding to know what Mum would have done had she got home and discovered there were weapons on her property. She wasn't in the mood for his moralising. 'Well, now that I've met you,' Mum replied after a moment's thought, 'I'm not so sure what I'd do.'

I laughed. I wanted to hug her for her bravery and her sense of humour. It gave me hope that she'd be all right. The intensity of this meeting was like nothing I'd ever experienced before. I had a real sense of this being a new and significant moment in our relationship.

On the Sunday morning, as I was being taken to an interrogation room, they invited me to look in the spy hole of another interrogation room. Approaching the door I didn't know who I was going to see. One of the IRA men who had called to my home was my first thought. I put my face up to the door and peered through the spy hole. There was Paddy, my little brother! I was horrified. At first I was alarmed by his body language. He was sitting on a chair, staring at the floor. I banged the door with my hand and shouted his name but couldn't think of anything to say. They dragged me away instantly. I could only pray he was remaining strong – and silent.

That Sunday afternoon a different detective came into the interview room and I was formally charged with possession of an AK47, a Springfield rifle, a Garand rifle and one other broken weapon. There were also two grenades, sixteen mercury tilt switches and over five hundred rounds of assorted ammunition. Just before they formally charged me they showed me each weapon one at a time. Each was individually wrapped in heavy, but see-through plastic.

'Have you ever seen this weapon before?' A detective in a suit held the AK47 out in front of his body. 'No reply,' his colleague would say each time, interpreting my silence. We repeated this process for all of the weaponry. They had one last sarcastic remark. 'Going to jail for shitty old weapons that don't work. One of these is from the First World War, for fuck's sake,' one said. Later, one of the interrogators came to my cell. He was short, overweight, wore steel-rimmed glasses and looked as if he had been going bald since his school days. He had been as polite as could be expected during the couple of interrogation sessions he sat in on.

'Tim?'

I looked around.

'You did the right thing. Good luck,' he said.

Mum and my family were all eventually released. I appeared briefly in court on Monday morning. There were several 'hoods' – ordinary criminals – in the holding cells with me. I avoided talking to them. Some of those around me talked about the fact that they would get bail and be out the next day or getting sentences that could be measured in weeks and months rather than years. The hours in their company proved to be an unforgettable lesson in the relative nature of time. Harsher lessons were just around the corner.

Killing Time

When you place a gun to a man's head and prepare to squeeze the trigger, expect the unexpected. Not everyone begs for mercy. A prisoner – I'll call him Joe – whom I met in Crumlin Road Prison found himself in exactly this situation – he was the shooter, not the shootee – and witnessed his victim display defiance bordering on derision.

This fascinated me, as it seemed to jar with what I had previously read – that when most men are about to die, they cry out for their mother. The mother–child bond is the unbreakable one, the intimate, defining one. We cry out for our mothers to help us the minute we're born, why not in the hour of our death? In the Crum I heard in gruesome detail how men reacted at the critical moment; as the getaway car's engine started to rev; as the safety catch was released; as the hammer struck the bullet in the chamber of the pistol pressed against the skull of the man whose number was up. Only once did it ever make me laugh.

The C Wing of Crumlin Road Prison had a canteen which was a deliberately featureless space. It was little more than four walls and an apex roof. It was a separate structure, built long after the Victorian prison, and connected to it by a small corridor. Institutional beige inside, it boasted Spartan furniture. Plastic patio chairs and tables, new and garishly white, served as riot-proof furniture. There were two showers just off the main hall, over in the corner, where we could wash – the whole place smelled of chips and soap. Aside from a TV bolted to the wall, the only remarkable feature of the room was a manned sentry post by the entrance. Behind toughened, darkened glass bored screws watched bored prisoners playing cards, watching the news or sitting in huddles chatting.

It was in one of these huddles that Joe shocked his captive audience. Men in football shorts and T-shirts begged him to tell them what the last words of his alleged victim were. Intrigued, I pulled up a chair. Joe showed little reticence about spilling the beans and quickly confirmed that something had been said to him by the man with the gun in his face; the dead man talking. 'I just couldn't believe what I was hearing,' Joe said. 'What did he say? What to fuck did he say before you whacked him?' one young prisoner demanded. Joe, looking at four or five breathless, eager faces, drew breath and then hesitated again on the cusp of his revelation. 'What did he say? Tell us for fuck's sake?' someone demanded. Joe spoke: 'He said: "You're going to shoot who, ye fucking fenian bastard?"'

The Crum was full of stories of such human drama. Human drama, death and, believe it or not, humour. We all laughed loudly at this story, not because we were indifferent to death, but because the victim's reaction was so unlikely. It took a second before I realised I was being taken for a ride. People deal with death and its consequences in any number of ways, and this includes the killers, not just those close to the victims. One prisoner on our wing was a much older man who, almost twenty years after shooting dead a British soldier, had handed himself in because he could not live with the guilt.

All those innocent victims, legitimate targets, the father-of-two, the 'Good Samaritans', the nun, the well-known loyalists, the heart-of-gold policeman, the innocent bystanders and recently arrived squaddies – all lives extinguished by the men on our wings, by the men in our yard and, occasionally, by the other man in my cell. I was soon to discover that, even as I awaited trial in jail, death would come so close it would scare the life out of me.

Those first weeks in the Crum in autumn 1990 were a culture shock. From the moment I was driven into the jail from the court after Castlereagh I had to start making major adjustments. On the first evening I was shown to the 'Basement' where all men spent their first night. I was told to strip and shower and, as I stood in the shower, a screw handed me some sort of delousing powder, which I thought a little excessive, even if I was a student. A sneering screw asked me if I wanted to go into B Wing with the ordinary criminals (drug-dealers, rapists and burglars) or if I wanted to join with the 'paramilitaries'? 'Wherever the republicans are,' I said. He gave a little snort of derision and said to his mate, 'Sad, isn't it? Really sad.'

Republicans were housed in both A and C Wings. Each had three landings known as the Ones, the Twos and the Threes. A screw made the often-heard call down the length of the cavernous corridor to his colleagues on the second floor: 'C two, one on!' This let the screws above know a new prisoner was on the way up and they should find him a cell.

The first few days were a blur. My first cellmate was a young guy in on non-IRA charges. He was getting bail the following day and I was shattered by his good fortune. It took some time for the reality to sink in. I kept thinking that someone would open the door and say: 'Right, Brannigan, there's been a terrible mix-up, you can go home.' Instead, they'd say: 'Slop out!' or 'Canteen'. Mostly though, they said nothing as they assumed that we all knew the drill, but of course I didn't.

I was told that lying in bed during the day wasn't the done thing. Some older prisoners folded up all bed sheets and blankets into a tidy bundle, which sat at the end of the bed until they were ready to sleep again that night. During the day, bed was for sitting on, not lying in. Apparently, this was how the IRA did their time in the past. Now, in the nineties, volunteers confronted this militaristic approach with more modern sensibilities. Some of the younger lads only ever knew Thatcher as the Prime Minister in Britain. They may have hated her but they were still influenced by the idea of 'rights', 'choice' and 'individuality'. This meant a slight disconnect between what the IRA asked us to do at times and what some new prisoners 'felt' like doing. Ultimately though, the IRA was not a 'democratic' army. They simply laid down the law and, with the odd murmur of discontent, men followed the 'Army line'.

The visits in those initial few days were frantic. The first was with Mum, trying to look cheery, and my younger brother Paddy. He laughed at my prison-issue shoes and I laughed along. It was one of the first genuine laughs I'd had in days. Soon though, we began speculating about who might have touted. We realised, or rather, Paddy had realised, very early on, that Martin Clarke, the young guy we had met in the street, had acted very suspiciously on the night I was arrested.

Clarke was, I believe, educationally subnormal and was often bullied by boys his age – he was seventeen years old when I was arrested. I always had time for him, even when many others in the area did not. He always called me Timothy – it seemed polite. When we stopped the car at the local sweet shop on the way to football, just after the IRA had left the weaponry, Clarke was inside making a phone call to the RUC, telling them what he had just witnessed at our house. We didn't realise that he had just made the call or what its impact would be for my family, the IRA or me. It was unfortunate for him that he had bumped into me and Paddy seconds after he had just betrayed us. By moving erratically at the shop doorway he had, inadvertently, drawn attention to himself. Standing out is a cardinal sin for any informer. They find safety in numbers; they aim to be unremarkable, ordinary.

Three friends came up to see me on the second of my three weekly visits, but with regulations only permitting two of them to enter, one went to the Front Page bar on the edge of the city centre to wait until the visit was over. Seamus, one of my closest friends, and Colly asked how the cops knew about the weapons. I recounted my version of events and mentioned what my brother had noticed about Clarke. After the visit, my friends made the short walk into town and, in a bizarre coincidence, just as they approached the Front Page, a car pulled up and Martin Clarke stepped out of a shop doorway. The car contained two RUC Special Branch men. They beckoned Clarke towards them. Perhaps, he was meeting them to receive money, a few hundred quid for putting me in jail and having the weapons seized. Perhaps he was receiving instructions on who his next target was to be. Whatever Special Branch had in store for him, his days as an informer were numbered . He just didn't know it.

Things moved quickly after that and the IRA arrested Clarke. He told them that he had been asked by Special Branch to watch out for known IRA volunteers and pass on information about their movements. Clarke was taken to a safe house and questioned. He was shot six times – in the arms, knees and ankles. The IRA explained to me their reasons for not shooting him dead. People have died for much less, but I was genuinely relieved that he wasn't killed. Clarke had had a tough life up to that point and he was little more than a pawn to the RUC had who risked his life to put me in jail. Besides, his getting killed wasn't going to alter my situation one bit. On the night he informed the cops, he had been sitting in a car that he had just bought when he spotted the IRA coming up our street. The car, a 'run-around', cost five hundred pounds and was paid for by Special Branch. It was payment for his services and to help him be more mobile for his spying. Not far from Clarke's house, on a wall, someone had written the warning: 'Touts will be shot.'

The OC (Officer in Command) of the IRA men in C Wing of Crumlin Road Prison had a warning for me: 'Tim, you are going to get dog's abuse from the loyalists when you go into the yard, OK? Fuck 'em! Let's go.' I was reassured by this display of leadership and attitude. Loyalists might have had me marked as an easy target but the IRA had my back covered and so, chest out, I walked out into the yard.

It would be hard to imagine a more bleak and gloomy place. The triangular-shaped space was squeezed between C Wing and B Wing. A high, grey wall made up the third side. After a lap or two of the perimeter, I was sure the loyalists looking down from their cells would say something. While bracing myself for that, I also had to get to know my new comrades. I recognised some faces, including several lads from my own area. Many other men from Derry, South Armagh and Tyrone were strangers to me. Some of them looked at me in a slightly bemused way. Eventually, the abuse did come from the loyalists, but only sporadically, and it didn't faze me.

On my second week in the jail, my eldest brother Ciaran, came to see me. By this stage the novelty of jail had worn off and I was, like everyone else, contemplating bigger issues. How was Mum doing? How long would I get? What age would I be when I got released? Ciaran, quite earnest compared to my other brothers, told me of an incident at home that I didn't know about. My solicitor had called to our home to brief them on my situation. He told my family that I had made a statement in Castlereagh. Making or signing statements in custody was not to be countenanced and those who did sign were often spoken about in less than complimentary terms. Ciaran said that my younger brother, Paddy, was angry – 'Our Tim would never make a statement!' he'd said. I felt like I had let him down. I realised my brother too was worried that I might have named names or let down the family.

I had felt that I had no option but to sign to help ensure that Mum got out of Castlereagh and that they didn't keep arresting members of my family. The cops had said they would arrest Ciaran, who at that time worked in Shorts, an aircraft factory in east Belfast with a mainly Protestant workforce. They threatened to arrest him at work, which would effectively have ended his job. After Ciaran's visit I went back to my cell a broken man and cried into a towel. Before long, the door opened and we were told to go to the canteen. I was in no mood for it. My cellmate insisted that I come down for association. I did so reluctantly.

Pádraic Wilson came up to see me on a visit around this

time. There were a few difficulties I needed to have sorted out. He was a man known to finesse complex or difficult situations. He had done time during the blanket protest himself and talked in a level-headed, pragmatic way about the dos and don'ts of jail. He had been briefed by someone on the outside regarding the circumstances that led to my arrest and re-counted to me what the IRA had told him about what went wrong. It was a more comprehensive account than I had pre-viously been given. Leaving, he simply advised that I now focus on the matter in hand. The matter in hand was putting my time in amid the squalor and tensions of the Crum.

The main problem with jail, for me at least, was the lack of privacy. We were locked in our cells twenty-one hours a day unless things were going badly, in which case we were locked up, two to a cell, for twenty-four hours a day. The cells had old wooden, drafty window frames and could be cold. I put time in listening to the radio, reading classic literature sent in by friends and family and reading the *Guardian*.

Letter writing was also a pleasure. I think most of the time friends were intrigued by everyday life in the jail and, at times, I would try to convey what it was like. Letters, however, could also be a source of conflict and could be used as an opportunity to inflict petty humiliations. From time to time, the screws would give one of us mail meant for a loyalist prisoner or vice versa. This may have been accidental, as a screw may not have been concentrating while sliding letters under our cell doors. It may, equally, have been vindictive. Often, the guy who got the misdirected mail would wait until after final lock-up at 7 p.m., then proceed to read it out loudly for the amusement of his comrades and to embarrass the intended recipient.

One day a guy showed me a letter that had been intended for a loyalist. At the time, the classic drama *Roots* was being repeated on TV. The wife of this loyalist prisoner had written the letter to her husband and signed off with, 'Well, that'll do for now. I have to go, as I want to see that nigger thing, *Roots*. It's great.' It didn't anger me, really. I just thought it ironic that the point of the show had sailed over her head.

On the last page of the letter the woman had let her child write a few words. They were the normal things that a child would say in such circumstances, but I was moved by the line: 'I miss you, daddy, and I sleep in your bed.' I felt slightly guilty for having read it.

The Northern Ireland Office insisted that the jail be run as a normal 'integrated' prison. They claimed that the loyalists and ourselves mixed freely and shared the same wings. It might have been more accurate to say we shared the same space, but never at the same time. We were placed in alternate cells. If two loyalists were in cell one, cell two would contain republicans, cell three, loyalists, and so on down the wing. The day began with the screws entering the wing rattling keys and cheerily shouting, 'Hands off cocks! Feet in socks!' The screws would then open all the loyalist cells to allow them to go to the canteen. While they were eating, we were allowed out to clean our cells, get showers and go to the toilet.

In January 1991, the screws moved about eight men from C Wing to A Wing with an equal number moving the other way. This small switch changed the atmosphere on the wing. For the first time since I arrived in the jail three months earlier, the wing was noisy at night with some of the new lads shouting jokes and insults up and down the wing. Barry McElduff, a bookish raconteur and now a Sinn Féin politician, regaled us with witty stories and quotations from the great and the good. Among the new faces was a man from Ardoyne in north Belfast called Jimmy McCleave. He was, as we used to say, a 'good chanter'. Someone asked Jimmy for a song. It was the first time I'd heard anyone sing in the jail and it was electric. Jimmy was a small guy, with thinning red hair and a hangdog expression. He had a booming voice and, for some reason, affected a southern Irish accent while singing. Perhaps he wanted a more 'authentic' Irish balladeer sound. As I lay on my bed listening to the chatter, Jimmy got up to his door and began to sing the old ballad, 'The Oul Triangle':

To begin the mornin', how the screws were bawlin'
Ah, get up ye bastards and clean out your cell ...
And the oul triangle goes jingle jangle
All around the banks of the Royal Canal

At the end of the song men 'got on their doors', kicking the metal and cheering loudly. This was one of the most exhilarating feelings I'd had up to that point and a part of me, in some romantic, idealised way, felt that we were part of a long line of Irish men who had resisted British rule. The loyalists never acted in this way. They didn't sing songs, they didn't chat as such. They seemed to either listen to us or shout sectarian slogans. I was glad they didn't sing as they only had three songs: 'God Save The Queen', 'The Sash' and 'Simply the Best' by Tina Turner. Their silence was probably for the best.

We observed an uneasy truce with the loyalists but some of their hot-headed members often acted unilaterally – republicans tended to be more disciplined. As the months went by we could see that the loyalists were getting extremely aggressive and in the spring of 1991 they began to attack us whenever they could. By the summer the jail was at breaking point. The IRA decided that the softly-softly approach was not working and the word went out for us to fight back. Actual hand-to-hand combat was infrequent, but not unheard of, and some of our lads relished the challenge. My record in hand-to-hand fights is a bit like the history of nationalist struggles against the British – too many glorious defeats for my liking. We were told to try and scald loyalists using hot water from the large water flasks that sat on each landing in case we wanted tea while cleaning out our cells. Loyalists were planning the same treatment for us.

It was my luck that one day as I was walking down the wing to have a shave, a loyalist was called in off the yard for the doctor's surgery. He would be passing below me in a matter of seconds. Our OC had been quite specific, 'Fuckin' get into them, lads – we need to create a crisis in the jail.' I knew that every man was aware that a republican was out on the landing with a loyalist about to pass below him. I didn't have a cup for hot water. Across the landing though, I could see that the cell of a Strabane republican was open. I ran round and said: 'There's a loyalist coming in off the yard, you can scald him.' My 'comrade' – as reluctant to go to the punishment block or 'the boards' as I was – pointed to the floor he had just mopped and said, 'But I'm cleaning my cell.' In a rare moment of bravado, I grabbed his cup from his cell and filled it with hot water. As the loyalist passed below me, I tipped it over the rail towards his head. I watched as the water cascaded from the cup, only then realising that it really was a long way down. I was surprised it hadn't turned to ice by the time it hit him. It caught the back of his head, shoulder and back.

'Brannigan!' a screw shouted. The screws raced towards me and the wing was 'locked down'. All movement in the jail was stopped, a standard security tactic in the event of trouble. I was marched off to 'the boards', where I served three days in a cell which contained exactly this: one metal bed frame bolted to the floor; one alarmingly stained blanket; one tiny, hardboard table; one white plastic chair; one bible. The tedium was broken only by the fact that my new accommodation overlooked the Crumlin Road itself, so if I clambered up to the window I could see traffic, people, nurses and doctors from the nearby hospital and a view of west Belfast – and home. The screws played Max Bygraves' *Greatest Hits* all day long. I did at least read the entire New Testament and, to entertain some of my comrades who were also on the boards, I decided to read out some of the more well-known extracts. I read the one often seen at sporting events and football matches, John 3:16. 'For God so loved the world, that He gave His only begotten Son, that whosoever believeth in Him should not perish, but have eternal life.'

When I was allowed back to the wing, it was the hottest day of the year. As I walked into the yard, the lads were soaking up the sun. 'Here's Cool Hand Luke' someone quipped and I felt very proud – not so much of trying to scald someone, but of not ducking out of the situation, of following the order and of 'doing my whack' in the expected manner.

Shortly after that, I was taken through the tunnel under Crumlin Road, which linked the jail to the courthouse on the opposite side of the road, for my arraignment. We made that journey once a month to be remanded in custody. It was a safer bet than taking us across the road, as escape was much less likely. I had heard about the tunnel and imagined it might be some ancient, dank place full of history and rats. I was disappointed to find that it was more like a service tunnel, with heating pipes running along the walls on both sides and pipes wrapped in silver foil. And, for a subterranean tunnel, it was very warm, like a hospital.

The arraignment is a legal process where the charges are formally read out in court. It gives prisoners their first chance to enter a plea of guilty or not guilty although it is not a full trial, more a legal formality. Most prisoners pleaded not guilty at this point and were sent back to the Crum. Had a prisoner pleaded guilty, however, he could have been sentenced on the spot without the need for a full trial. I was told that if I pleaded guilty I could be sentenced and up in the Blocks, out of the mess that was the Crum. It was 4 July 1991, the last day of the court session before the long summer recess.

The previous day, several leading loyalists including west Belfast UDA Commander Tommy 'Tucker' Lyttle, his son Tommy 'Tucker' Junior and Eric McKee, were sentenced for having photo montages and security force documents used to target republicans and nationalists. They were sentenced to seven, five and six years respectively. Some of them had been in jail previously.

Yet, the very same judge, twenty-four hours later, said that if I pleaded guilty I would receive twelve years and should count myself 'lucky'. 'I can't be seen to be lenient in terrorist cases,' he claimed, somewhat implausibly. My barrister said I would be foolish to plead guilty for twelve as I was probably 'only' looking at fifteen years maximum, anyway. A benchmark had been set for the length of time I was likely to get. So no deal was made that day and all I could do was walk through the tunnel back to the Crum.

The low-level attacks and aggression of the loyalists began to reach a crescendo and our response had, to that point, been muted. When loyalists on the outside shot at a minibus carrying relatives of some of our lads to the prison for a visit murmurs that 'something had to be done' grew to a chorus. We genuinely feared that one of us, or worse, one of our visitors, would be killed. The IRA decided to hit back and, as ever, hit hard – it was just a question of when. The OC made the situation brutally clear; someone was going to get killed. At the time, I thought they were warning us to watch out for each other in case of loyalist attack. In retrospect, there was an element of this but I now realise, too, that they were making a statement of intent.

Night after night in a prison cell is a search for simple pleasures and an even more futile quest for privacy. In a space designed for one and occupied by two, it was a losing battle. With the last lock-up at 7 p.m. exactly, long, empty evenings stretched out before us. I had just graduated from college in Liverpool and many of the men I found myself in jail with had left school at sixteen. We probably wouldn't have had each other as ideal cellmates, given a choice, but then the defining feature of jail is the lack of choice. An ability to compromise on the basics of living was essential and, while there were occasional rows, a willingness to cooperate was the key to relatively harmonious living. A focal point to the evening was often a pre-bedtime feast. If we were ambitious, it involved making toast. In a cell without electric, gas, a cooker, a toaster or even a power point ingenuity was needed.

To make toast in Crumlin Road Jail you need four slices of bread, a knob of the foul-tasting 'butter-flavoured' spread and a plastic butter knife. You also need lots of toilet roll; an army-style camp bed with a metal frame; a wastepaper bin, also metal; an empty milk carton and a petrol lighter. It does not matter whether you smoke or not, you should always own a lighter in jail. Now, fold your mattress back upon itself to expose the metal springs of the bedstead. Turn the bin upside down and place it under the springs. Take long strips of toilet roll and twist them into tight little clumps about the size of a decent pork sausage. Place some of the twisted up loo roll on top of the bin and light it. Position the bread above the flame until toasted. Make sure the rubber-covered mattress doesn't catch fire because the Crumlin Road screws, at least while I was there, didn't seem to understand the concept of rapid response. Some lads smeared the loo paper with butter, making it burn harder, but this meant that the smoke, which was inevitably going to fill the cell for the next hour, would be even more acrid and choking than normal.

Having made the toast, tea was made in the same way. Using the same method as before, water was heated in either an empty Marvel (powdered milk) tin or, more usually, in a milk carton. The wax on the milk carton meant that it did not burn and was able to withstand the quite intense flames long enough to boil the water. I didn't believe it would work and thought it was a ruse to get me to make an idiot of myself as a burning carton shed its contents onto my floor. Discovering that it was yet another piece of prisoner ingenuity was a little epiphany.

But the denial of privacy was frustrating at times. Not only did we have cellmates, we also had regular checks from screws peeking in the spy hole in the door. When I first arrived in the Crumlin Road jail, a friend in England sent me a copy of *The Gulag Archipelago* by Aleksandr Solzhenitsyn. A screw brought it to my cell and asked who bought it for me. I said it was from a college friend in England. The screw suddenly put on a very camp, effeminate voice and said, 'Ooh, my college friend in England, la-di-da.' Some of the lads found this funny and, I guess, to some extent, this shaped their views of me, for better or worse. Indeed, I used this image to comedic effect on occasion. I joked to the screws on a regular basis that I was 'really not cut out for long-term imprisonment'.

The first time a cellmate, a man whom I hardly knew, told me he needed to go to the toilet, I assumed he was having a laugh. He wasn't. If you were lucky, your bowel movements chimed nicely with the occasions on which you were allowed out of the cell. When showering, going to the yard or going on a visit, a quick dash to the loo might be facilitated. After 7 p.m. we were confined to our cells and at the mercy of our digestive system. Inevitably nature called. We each had a plastic chamber pot for all toilet needs. Peeing in the pot was acceptable, but having a shit, to use the vernacular, and then letting that sit in the cell all night was categorically out. Ingenuity was needed, so republican prisoners nicked an idea from the seventeenth century when it came to waste disposal. The ritual involved lining the waste-paper bin with the large brown paper bags we were given to put our dirty laundry in. The bin was placed by the door. Then we simply sat on the bin and proceeded to do our business. Disposing of the waste was a ritual. Whoever had used the bin would carefully lift the bag out, close it slightly and stand on the bed below the window so that he could reach out and fling it into the yard below. Some of the lads would shout, 'Mystery parcel!' or 'Parcel from America!' as they launched the package. I, in contrast, would try to get the noisy rustling, brown bag through the bars outside my window as quietly as possible, so that the men in neighbouring cells didn't hear me. I worried that men would discover that I'd just been to the toilet.

Around October 1991, I was sent from C Wing to A Wing. It was a bigger wing, considered more secure and it contained a couple of 'Red Books' (maximum-security prisoners). Overnight, and for the first time in a year, I had about seventy new faces to look at; new men, new personalities, new slaggings and banter. I shared a cell with Tony Millar, an experienced republican from Derry and an easy man with whom to do time. He had faced a murder charge before and had been cleared. This time, having been arrested by the SAS, he was facing possession of explosives charges.

One Sunday evening we sat in our cell getting newspapers and tea sorted out before the final lock-up. Tony seemed more concerned than usual about having music, water, crisps and other essentials in the cell. We small talked and flicked through the papers, him on his bed and me on a white plastic chair. Only the loyalists, enjoying the last few minutes of their evening association in the canteen, had to be locked up and then the screws would head home, leaving a skeleton night staff. I was rocking back on the chair's two rear legs, leaning against the cell door, when there was a thunderous bang. I thought it was a rocket attack on the British Army lookout post at the front of the jail. Within seconds all hell broke loose. Shouting rang out from the loyalists. A din of sirens, panic and barked orders among the screws filled the wing while we remained quiet, trying to work out what the hell was going on. I had no idea what had happened. The radio news eventually confirmed to us that there had been an IRA bomb *inside* C Wing canteen as loyalists had gathered for evening association. It was hidden behind the radiator and when it went off the radiator was ripped apart and shrapnel sliced through air, flesh and bone. Two loyalists were killed. One of them was arrested on the same night as me for trying to murder a Catholic nurse in north Belfast – he and his gang had beaten her with a wheel brace before attempting to abduct her. I was surprised but not totally shocked by the bomb, such was the brutalising effect of jail.

The loyalists began issuing death threats. Sometimes we laughed these off but deep down we had concerns that loyalists would either strike against us or worse, against our families. I wondered if the screws would don riot gear and beat the crap out of us. Tony speculated that 'the heads', the republican leaders in the jail and any big names, might be taken out of the Crum and flown by helicopter to the H-blocks. He was partly correct – men were moved, but instead of sending them to the H-blocks they simply moved all the men in C Wing to A Wing and vice versa. Only four men in the jail didn't move. The four exceptions were the three men on Red Books – as maximum-security prisoners they had to remain in A Wing – and me. I joked that I was clearly considered to be a threat and had to be kept with the Red Book lads.

The jail was on twenty-four-hour lock-up. We weren't even allowed to go to the toilet or wash for the first week or so. We peed in our pots until they were overflowing. Just by the entrance, the cell floor sloped down towards the metal door, so we left our pots by the door and any overspill ran onto the landings. Screws in boiler suits and white face masks pushed a bin along the landing on a trolley and we were told to empty our brimming pots into the bin. The same screws then came back minutes later with our freezing dinner on paper plates. The OC told us to start hurling the piss pots rather than gently pouring them when the bin came around. The aim was to make a splash that would soak the screws. When my cell door opened, the screws, two of the sorriest looking specimens I'd ever seen, were trying to step away from the bin. I could tell by their boiler suits that some lads must have gone for the screws rather than the bin. I hadn't the heart to throw it at them but I was determined to follow the order. I hurled my piss for all I was worth and scored a direct hit pretty much in the centre of the bin, which was filled to overflowing. The piss splashed in all directions. The screws got hit, my cell floor got hit and some of it hit me in the face and hands. I tried to look hard and hoped they didn't notice I had suffered serious splashback in the whole episode. Beyond caring and with their shoulders slumped, they slowly trundled their unwanted cargo to the next cell in silence. I sat on my bed and wiped myself down with a towel and threw water on my face.

I was given a new cellmate, a man from a rural area. I'll call him 'Sean'. It would be fair to say that we saw the world differently, although he was a very likeable guy. Sean had a big family and they often wrote to Downtown Radio for requests for him and 'all the lads' in A Wing. At night he would talk about his family and life in the town. I asked him what the little mark was on the side of his eye, near his temple. It was a tan mark and I therefore expected him to confirm it was a birthmark.

'Oh, that? That's a tea stain,' he said.

'You what?' I exclaimed.

'It's a tea stain I got when me ma spilled a cup of tea on herself while she was pregnant with me.'

I laughed out loud and saw him get angry as I suggested it was just an old wives' tale. I think he just never thought to challenge the truth of this yarn at any stage in his life. Indignant, he pulled up his sleeve and, in a challenging tone, said, 'And what about these, then? Are they just an old wives' tale, too?' There were two little lumps of skin no bigger than match heads. I asked what they were and he said: 'Rat's tits'. I laughed even harder than before, asking what he was on about. 'When my ma was pregnant with me she was bitten by a female rat and I got the "rats tits" mark on my arm,' he said. An eventful pregnancy all around, then, if his sisters are to be believed, I thought. I decided not to challenge this family legend.

And so, with tall tales, bombs, riots, death and attacks, Irish independence clashed with British justice twenty-four hours a day and, in Crumlin Road jail, several hundred men pleasured Her Majesty every single night. It was with some relief, then, that my solicitor told me I had a date for trial. It was to happen on one of the last court days before Christmas 1991. Unlike the previous 4 July date, this time I was told that I could receive 'ten years with leeway', according to my barrister. She and I had had a brief meeting where I told her about the IRA's attitude to pleading guilty. Primarily, it was because the IRA did not want their men to accept the tag of 'criminal', which by pleading guilty they did, to some extent. It certainly legitimised the process.

However, the IRA was powerless once individuals crossed over to the court. Then hard-nosed, seen-it-all-before lawyers, as well as our families, wives, friends and natural human self-interest took over and prisoners had a short time in which to decide whether to be 'staunchers' and plead not guilty or take a deal and get a few years off. My barrister told me if I took the deal I was probably looking at seven or eight years having already served fourteen months. To be honest, I didn't need persuading. I simply worked out what age I'd be when I got released.

As with the arraignment on 4 July, lecturers from my university who had flown over from Liverpool and Pat McCann, my A-level teacher, all spoke on my behalf. The judge, Hutton, seemed impressed and permitted Pete Gill – my former politics lecturer, and something of an expert when it came to policing – to have an impromptu visit with me in the cells below the court.

As with the first night in the Crum, after sentencing, prisoners are sent to the basement of the jail. Here, isolated from the other prisoners, I was given the chance to sever all links and serve my term in the mixed Maghaberry prison with ordinary criminals. Some chance. I was much more assertive than I had been on my arrival. When asked what jail I wanted to go to, I said, 'The Blocks, of course,' with a smile. I also walked around like I owned the place, moving at my pace, not theirs, and I made some wisecracks. They let me out to 'slop out'. As I walked into the toilet area, I instantly recognised a man doing the same thing. It was Pádraic Wilson.

A day or two before I was sentenced the IRA left a massive bomb at Lurgan RUC station in County Armagh. The devastation at the barracks was matched only by that sustained by a local primary school. Several large bombs had gone off around that time and the IRA was stretching the Brits and cops to breaking point. RUC Chief Constable Hugh Annesley was questioned about the 'upsurge' in IRA activity by the press and, in response, mentioned that his officers were having successes of their own. As he spoke, Annesley claimed that two 'top-quality terrorists' were being questioned in Castlereagh. I had heard this on the radio. It was only now that I realised that the 'terrorists' he had been referring to were Jim 'Flash' McVeigh and Pádraic Wilson who had been caught on active service. I asked Pádraic what had happened and he said he'd been caught making a bomb. I asked what the prospect of beating the charge was. 'Fucked,' he said, casually.

'What's it like on the wings?' he asked.

'It's calming down but it's grim, like ...'

I paced my cell for hours, singing to express my euphoria at a short sentence, seven years, fourteen months of which I had already served on remand. I found it best to see my situation relative, that of other people in the struggle. Pádraic, Flash and another volunteer, Tony O'Neill, were in jail because someone touted on them. The tout was shot dead soon after. Pádraic and Flash were later to get twenty-four years each and young Tony O'Neill got eighteen years.

In 2008 I found a prayer Mum had written while I was in the Crum:

Dear Jesus, please help my son, Timothy. He needs you. Show him how powerful you are. Touch him now, now in his hour of trouble. Make his period of waiting go quickly and his trial a fair one. I am hopeful of your help as you and you alone are the one who can see into his heart. His life has not been the easiest. I have been especially hard on him and I am sorry. Forgive me. I beg the Holy Mother to guide and comfort my lovely son. Thy will be done. Amen.

6041

The first thing I noticed about the H-blocks was the respect that the screws showed us. There wasn't the same cockiness from them as there had been from the screws when I entered the Crum. As I walked onto wing H4, Danny Morrison, former Sinn Féin Publicity Director, came towards me smiling: 'Good timing, we've got gallons of drink brewing for New Year's Eve.'

Just after I arrived, I was taken to a cell for an induction and orientation briefing; a quite formal process which had several elements to it. The IO (Intelligence Officer) brought me to his cell and produced a small map of architect's plans of the jail, drawn to scale. They looked as though they had been professionally drafted on the outside and showed the pitches, the eight H-blocks and the visit area in exacting detail and to scale. The map was designed to help me get my bearings within the camp. It showed that the IRA took things seriously and it gave me an insight into how much the IRA knew about my new world.

My first few visits with Mum were fraught. She was conflicted over my seven-year sentence. She realised I could have been hit with worse but she also now knew that the possibility of my walking away with a suspended sentence had gone. She got annoyed when she saw the high walls and lookout posts during her visits.

'Those watchtowers and all the grey steel and all that barbed

wire would bring anyone down. Are you going to be OK in here?
Sometimes I ... Well, I wish none of this had ever happened.'

'Mum, we've been over all of this ...'

She looked away and took deep gulps of air. I reached across
the table and held her hand, 'Don't cry, Mum ...'

Some people described the H-blocks as a 'holiday camp'. It
was also described as a 'university of terror' by unionists,
Tories and some in the media. In their fevered imaginations it
was a place where we trained in terror tactics; where we
organised 'outrages'. No, the truth was more humdrum, less
deadly. Compared to any other jail republicans may have
found themselves in, the IRA wings of the Blocks were a
remarkable place. Years of struggle by the IRA prisoners eventually won them freedoms unrivalled anywhere else in Europe.
But the price to be paid for such privileges was a heavy one.
Ten men died so that prisoners could do their time with some
dignity. The H-blocks were another front in the IRA's war
against the British. It was an unarmed front – mostly – in a
politicised war of attrition. We wouldn't let up, we wouldn't
give in and, ultimately, we wouldn't be beaten.

By the time I got to the H-blocks it was a very different jail
from that experienced by the protesting 'blanketmen' and
hunger strikers of the late 1970s and early 1980s. It was all very
civilised with a laid-back regime that suited almost everyone.
The screws had to ask for the IRA's permission if they wanted
to come down the wings. Eventually they treated the wings as
a virtual no-go area although they were never threatened or
harmed. Sometimes they would open the gate, pop their head
round and ask to speak to our OC. Running the wings was often
a negotiation between the prison authorities and the IRA.
However, we were still locked in our cells at night to do our
sentence, and when the cell door slammed behind us, we were
left to think about our families, our friends and our futures.

The H-blocks were built by the British in the 1970s, as a place
that would break the republican struggle by criminalising it.
The blocks replaced the 'cages', the old Nissan huts that

housed IRA prisoners who had been afforded 'special category', effectively political, status. In the early 1970s, the IRA was viewed by the British government as being politically motivated. Prisoners had special category status and could wear their own clothes and associate freely with their comrades. The IRA command structure was recognised by the prison authorities and, by extension, by the British government. Republicans were effectively prisoners of war. And then everything suddenly changed. The British decided that no liberal democracy could be seen to be fighting a war so close to home. It was bad PR. As a result, it was decided that the prisoners should be treated as ordinary criminals and forced to wear prison clothes and do prison work. It was announced that from 1 March 1976 anyone convicted of a 'scheduled offence' would no longer qualify for special status. They would not go to the cages but would serve their time in the new H-blocks as criminals. Republican prisoners resisted and refused to wear the prison uniform. Rather than stand naked in their cells they wrapped themselves in their blankets and so the protest was born. They were refused access to the toilets and so had to defecate in their cells. Initially they threw the waste out of the cell windows but the screws got petty criminals in protective clothing to come around and throw the shit back in the windows, often as prisoners lay sleeping: 'Worst thing about it was that the shit that came back through your window was often someone else's shit,' said Seanna 'Sid' Walsh, a former cellmate of mine. Then the screws blocked up the windows leaving the prisoners with little choice but to spread it on the walls. There were practical considerations; it meant the prisoners wouldn't be lying in it and, on the walls, it dried out quicker. The prisoners lived in these deplorable conditions for four years before embarking on a hunger strike to force a conclusion to their protest and to win the right to be political prisoners. The first hunger strike in late 1980 ended as the life of one hunger striker hung in the balance, when a deal was promised by the British government. It proved to be a stalling exercise. A second hunger strike, led by Bobby Sands, began on 1 March 1981. Despite Bobby Sands getting elected to the British Parliament halfway through his strike, in April 1981, British Prime Minister Maggie Thatcher chose to ignore the democratic mandate and allowed Sands to die. Nine more young Irish republicans died in the months after.

After a five-year 'dirt' (never dirty) protest and two hunger strikes, the Republican movement had had its fill of distracting, jail-related struggles. The IRA leadership and Sinn Féin started to look at the world with a heightened awareness of the potential of political and electoral successes. The IRA scaled down its attacks on prison officers on the outside after the hunger strikes and a non-violent strategy to resolve jail disputes was initiated. The prisoners decided to fight their own battles by peaceful means, lobbying the governors, writing to newspapers, and other low-level forms of agitation.

The jail, probably to the relief of both the British government and the IRA leadership, was becalmed and a regime of permanent crisis had become so relaxed that by 1983 the IRA was able to exploit the situation in spectacular fashion with an escape that was breathtaking in its ambition. They took control of H7 one Sunday in September having plotted and planned the escape over the preceding two years. They managed to get thirty-eight men smuggled to the front gate in a food van but their audacious plan to drive off down the road to the Republic and relative safety was thwarted when a screw raised the alarm. Although nineteen men were captured either near the prison perimeter or in nearby towns over the first hours and days, the other nineteen escaped.

A new extremely repressive jail regime was installed. Rules were aggressively observed; prisoner privileges were routinely denied. The men petitioned and campaigned the governors to grant small, incremental changes but for years the response was glacial. However by the late 1980s changes did come and they began to come at a quicker rate during my time there. Multigyms were placed on each wing; the range of items for sale in the shop increased; yards were allowed to stay open for longer and the movement of prisoners between wings was eventually permitted.

The H-blocks were built to a design that was meant to make it hard for the IRA to organise. There were no long wings holding hundreds of men like those found in Victorian jails such as Crumlin Road or Pentonville in England, which were the blueprint for many British jails. Instead, small wings, which were easily isolated from each other, were meant to fracture and frustrate ideas of a central command. Riots could be isolated and neutralised more easily from the screws' perspective. Each wing had twenty-four cells and during my years there we usually had our own cell with no need to share. Each man had a piece of square white card outside his cell door that displayed his name, date of birth and sentence received. It also gave each man's prison number. My own was 6041. The key detail was the release date on which we all focussed. Those convicted of killings or attempted killings weren't given a date and received an indeterminate sentence. Instead of a release date, their cards simply had the word 'Life'. Rarely has such a positive word carried with it such negative connotations.

I focused on little landmarks such as my birthday, New Year's Eve and the anniversary of my arrest so that I could chalk off weeks, months and years in small chunks. The pace of life was slower in the Blocks than the Crum so it was up to prisoners to generate their own dynamic into each day otherwise life became a neverending expanse of time spent in very restricted space. Secure in the belief that they had the whole jail nailed down, the authorities retreated from the wings and allowed us full control of a small area.

The IRA's response to attempts to break its influence in the H-blocks was to organise the men into what they called 'the commune'. Its very existence was a challenge to the prison authorities. It gave a socialist, collective ethos to every aspect of our lives. Daily life was organised to make things easy in a practical sense. Cell doors opened at 8.30 a.m. Each man was given a pint of milk per day. We all donated half the milk per carton into a metal urn, and filled the rest of the urn with water, making a weakened milk that was passable for tea drinking; tea being the drug of choice for most of us. The other half carton was given to each prisoner for their cereal or to drink as they saw fit. Those who liked to lie-in often found their carton gone when they got up. This was a source of constant squabbles, 'It's a sad day in this jail when prisoners can't be trusted, lads,' one man said earnestly when the milk for his cornflakes was 'stolen'. But perhaps men throwing their teabags into the sink rather than in the bins was the greatest source of conflict on the wings. Meetings were called to eradicate the scourge; names were named.

We all received a small jail wage of about three pounds from the authorities. This was pooled by every man on the wing so that the commune could buy coffee, tea, chocolate, tobacco and other essentials, which were held in a central 'dump'. Men who had no money or who ran out of tobacco could borrow from the dump on credit until their relatives next left in some money. Paying back was essential if the system was to work. It was equitable and egalitarian. If men were really stretched, economically, and some were, the commune discreetly provided them with what they needed. We were working-class men and our families couldn't always afford to leave money into the shop for us to spend on sweets, crisps and CDs. The commune and the fact that the IRA would underwrite its sanctions meant that theft from our cells was extremely rare, an almost unheard of event. I can't recall an incidence of it on any wing I was on. The ethos was collective. At one of the first meetings I was at, the OC reacted when one prisoner called another a 'bastard' during some petty dispute. 'Hold on here lads. There are no bastards or cunts or fuckers on these wings,' he told us. 'We are IRA prisoners. We don't all have to love each other but there must be respect. Remember who you are and what you represent …'

The IRA's determination to get men to use their time wisely, to educate themselves, to read, to study, to question, was impressive. Such an approach helped men discover their potential, even in such a hostile environment. The overt military trappings of the 1970s were discarded. Debate and discussion were actively encouraged and an education officer was appointed on each wing. Many of the men studied for and acquired Open University degrees. Many more studied for A levels and GCSEs. I attended courses on creative writing, drama and women's studies and I finally passed my maths GCSE in the Blocks, too. I also studied for A levels in English and French. There were endless discussions and debates of an informal nature about republican and Irish history and there was even a series of compulsory classes on the issue of forensic science. The latest advances in the field, including the rising trend of using DNA evidence to secure convictions, were discussed. It demonstrated impressive forward planning and attention to detail on the IRA's part.

While there were often valid requests for improvements to our quality of life, I imagine this would be true of prisoners in any jail. Many of us liked a good whinge, myself included. It helped let off a bit of steam: the burgers were too small; the visits were too short; the screws were too tight. Prison food was a major source of discontent. We considered jail food a cruel, unusual punishment, a human rights abuse. It was possible to wile away an idle moment watching men try to identify what on earth they were eating. They would tuck into their meal, chew for a second, stop suddenly, pull a face and then walk over to check what it said on the rudimentary menu taped to the wall. Complaining was futile. Gordon Ramsay could have been doing the cooking but by the time it was packed into the boxes, taken for a drive around the camp, unpacked and served, it was dire. I ruled out half the meals before they even reached the wing, making up the shortfall with toast, crisps, sandwiches and biscuits.

The IRA had an insatiable appetite for information about the jail and its staff. They used screws, priests, doctors, contractors, teachers, suppliers, governors, prisoners, loyalists, welfare staff and visitors. Every scrap of information was funnelled back to the IOs where its significance was analysed and scrutinised, discussed and debated for even the slightest advantage. Men on each wing pumped the screws for information every single day. Sometimes it was with direct questions but more often it was quite subtle. The screws discussed their petty work-related jealousies, their drink and gambling problems and their chronic low morale. And the IRA was always there offering them a non-judgemental shoulder to cry on.

Apart from the weekly visits, getting down to the 'big pitch' for eleven-a-side football was undoubtedly the highlight of the week for many men. The pitches, two gravelly, leisure-centre style rectangles surrounded by thirty-feet high wire security fences, were as close to wide-open space as we ever experienced. We could express ourselves using a bit of competitive edge and adrenalin although, with striking irony, the IRA banned us from ever getting violent. I loved to play centre forward and, in what was often an emotional release, I celebrated my goals as if I'd just helped Liverpool win another Champions League final. 'What to fuck is he playing at?' Alec Murphy was rolling up another fag, Brendan 'Bik' McFarlane was adjusting the sweatbands on his head and wrists that he had made from the prison-supplied towels and two men were claiming that the goal was 'off-fuckin'-side'.

Republicans weren't the only men in the jail. There were also a couple of hundred loyalists. In some blocks, they would occupy C and D Wings, while we were on A and B on the other side. The loyalists had a very different ethos from us. Their philosophy for doing time was influenced by the communities from which they sprang. We, the republicans, generally speaking, shared one faith, one aim – a united Ireland – and a common experience in facing the brutality of the British Army and decades of unionist misrule. All of this informed our worldview. The loyalists were much more factional. They belonged to at least four different religious denominations, from the relatively liberal Church of Ireland to the fundamentalist Free Presbyterians of Ian Paisley's self-styled church. Whereas the IRA controlled our wings, the loyalists observed leadership from the Ulster Freedom Fighters (UFF), Ulster Volunteer Force (UVF) and, to a lesser extent, the Red Hand Commando (RHC). Protestants, historically, had less of a sense of community or certainly of communal action. At various junctures in Irish history any idea of collective action with working-class Catholics was denounced from Protestant church pulpits as 'socialism', 'bolshevism' and, of course, republicanism. The loyalists were influenced by a Protestant upbringing that stressed *individual* responsibility and self-reliance. They prided themselves on their Protestant work ethic – although since historically nationalists were systematically barred from even taking jobs in banking, the civil service, the shipyard and the police force, perhaps this 'work ethic' amounted to little more than state-sponsored nepotism. That's how it seemed to me, at any rate. The men across the block also seemed to adhere to a self-serving notion of 'loyalty'; one which offered loyalty to the British Crown and the Queen but certainly not to the British government. It was a highly qualified loyalty. The brutalising effect of the war and the coarsening effect of Thatcherism meant that for loyalists there really was no such thing as society, simply survival of the fittest. This perhaps explains the loyalist paramilitary caricatures who exploited the cult of personality for personal prestige and gain. It is also why they would ultimately fall from power in a series of murderous feuds.

The loyalist prisoners also resented the fact that they were being locked up by people they regarded as 'their own'. The screws who locked the cell doors at night often came from the same streets as the loyalist prisoners. They went to the same churches, saluted the same flags and bent their knee to the same queen. This led to endless tensions between loyalist prisoners and their captors. It was no surprise, then, that most screws preferred to work on republican wings away from the loyalists, mainly because we did not humiliate the screws as loyalists prisoners often did.

Once a year, if we were on the same block as loyalists, we offered to swap our books with them. We filled boxes and heavy-duty paper bags with Shakespeare and Joyce, F. Scott Fitzgerald and the War Poets. On one particular occasion we added *The Communist Manifesto*, Frantz Fanon's *The Wretched of the Earth*, *The Ragged Trousered Philanthropists* as well as the inexplicably popular – to my mind anyway – Roddy Doyle trilogy. There were endless history books and books of political analysis as well as textbooks from the many OU and A-level courses. Copies of *Catch 22* and *Portnoy's Complaint* were sent to their wings. After a while a single box of Jeffrey Archer and Robert Ludlum novels was sent back to us. They had few books of any literary merit, nothing offering any analysis of the society in which they lived; no poetry. They seemed to read, if they read at all, airport novels and the collected writings of Jackie Collins.

We got some days in with idle chat. One day, sitting bored in a cell a prisoner from a rural area said: 'I just think it's unfortunate that a guy like you ended up in the Blocks.'

'What do you mean a guy like me?' I asked

'Well, it's not really your fight,' he stated, like it was a self-evident truth.

'I grew up on the Falls Road and I've probably had more abuse from the Brits than most people on these wings. I have a fair idea what's going on politically,' I said.

'But it's not really your fight,' he said.

'Certainly feels like I've been in a fight,' I said, getting up to go to the yard before he patronised me any further. Several IRA men from rural areas told me they had never seen a black man in their village or town. I didn't doubt it.

'Do you know what your problem is, Tim?' said a comrade, 'You're too sensitive.' This assessment came after an incident in which a teacher with a South American background and brown skin had come onto our block to teach a class only to hear men laugh at a race-based 'joke'. It was hardly a major racist comment and I never claimed it was but I knew the teacher to be a socialist and progressive in his thinking. I felt we were letting ourselves down and I knew the man who made the remark to be better than such silly stereotyping so I calmly told him that what he had said was embarassing and that it had reflected badly upon us. In fact, I rarely mentioned race but as an issue it did occasionally surface.

An old priest came in to say mass one Sunday. I sat at the back of the cell with about a dozen other prisoners in the room. When everything was ready for mass, the priest finally started to look around the room and slowly considered us with a smile. As his gaze stopped and fixed on me, he said, 'What in God's name are you doing here?' I didn't feel like defending my presence but during the mass I resolved to tell him a bit about myself when it was over.

Compared to life on the outside, the H-blocks were the least racist place I've ever been. The men weren't perfect and male prisons are home to some cutting humour and caustic remarks. The odd comment, usually originating from genuine ignorance rather than race hatred, was made and men were often quick to accept that they may have been out of order. 'Should I describe you as black or coloured?' asked one comrade. No one ever made a direct hostile attack on me because of my colour, they would not have been allowed to. One lifer sat a few rows in front of me as we crowded around the TV for a live FA Cup tie. Manchester United was playing Sheffield United. This prisoner was loudly and confidently predicting the score before the match had kicked off and he seemed to enjoy having an audience. He was unaware that I had taken my seat behind him. Just before the kick off, the camera focused on Brian Deane, a black, unshaven centre forward, playing for Sheffield: 'He just looks like a mugger, doesn't he?' A comrade and close friend of mine rolled his eyes, which was without doubt the most fitting response. Waiting for people to laugh at his observation the lifer glanced around and found me looking back at him. He went silent briefly and then began to lavish praise on any simple pass or tackle any black player made for the entire match. That was as rough as it ever got.

The only time I was called a 'nigger' or a 'black bastard' was by the loyalists on remand. I can't think of another maximum-security jail where this would have been the case and that is one of the principal reasons why, in recalling those days, I use the words 'comrade' and 'comrades'. I can't imagine any other jail where I would have felt so safe, so accepted.

The prison regime, no matter how quiet the jail appeared, had to observe basic security protocols and so, once a fortnight, there was a block search. The cry, '*Sin fir cuardach isteach*', rang out from the lads. It meant, simply, 'That's the search team in.' My heart would sink upon hearing this as I would often be asked to 'bangle' something. This innocuous phrase meant hiding highly sensitive, illegal IRA contraband up my bum until the search was over. I would agree and be handed some Vaseline in a tub and a sock with something hard in it. The IRA tried not to write too much down but it was unavoidable in jail. Everything was written down on cigarette papers. The writing was probably about the size of the letters on the buttons on the average mobile phone; fine ballpoint pens were used to aid clarity. I usually used two or three 'big skins', Rizla papers. These would be stuck together edge to edge to form a page and then the writing would begin. When finished, the 'comm' (communication) was folded in half several times into a little brick shape the size of a small piece of chewing gum. IRA comms could contain anything: escape plans; speculation about the identity of an informer; details of screws who were working for the IRA; the names of people who had carried out operations on the outside. Security was paramount. Bundles of comms were often bound together tightly in plastic bread wrappers making them too big to be hidden in our mouths so the only safe place was up our bums. The search teams went through the motions and inevitably they found nothing. They tended to leave after two hours and when they did we went to the toilets, and passed the package back out, removed some layers of the protective plastic and returned them to their rightful owners.

After a year or so, I was sent to H6 from H4. Different

blocks had different atmospheres. H4 was more relaxed with a lot more jokers and a high ratio of Belfast men. My arrival was, for one particular reason, greeted with near universal delight up in H6 – I was the jail barber on account of my three years working as a hairdresser and the lads were glad of proper haircuts.

Days drifted into weeks and months and we sat around shooting the breeze, so to speak. I was lying on a makeshift sofa in front of the TV. It was one of those endless grey days when inspiration and motivation were in short supply. I stopped day dreaming and began to listen to a conversation between Alex Murphy – who was serving life for the deaths of the two corporals that the IRA shot after they were captured and beaten at Kevin Brady's funeral in 1988 – and Pat 'Sheeky' Sheehan, a former hunger striker. Permanently dressed in tracksuits and leisure wear, Sheeky was tall and younger than Alex, who looked, even after several years in jail, as if he still wasn't getting enough rest.

'I don't believe you!' said Sheeky.

'I'm fuckin' tellin' ye,' said Alex, an incredulous smile on his face. 'They had both types.'

'What are you talking about?' I asked

'I'm just telling Sheeky that the Ra in Belfast had two types of warheads for the RPGs.'

He was talking about Rocket Propelled Grenades. 'Two types?' I asked.

'One was for going through masonry so you can fire them at the lookout posts in army bases. The other was for piercing the armour plating of jeeps and Saracens,' Alex explained.

'Well, I wish to fuck, someone had told me all this when I was out,' Sheeky said.

It was idle small talk – some might say loose talk – from two players who had been removed from the game. As small talk goes it was pretty incendiary. We went for a 'dander' around the yard.

In 1993, I was surprised to be approached by a prisoner who

had a little job for me. 'Tim, we were wondering if you'd ever thought of being the block OC?'

'Not really, to be honest,' I said.

'We think you'd be good for the role.'

'Must be because of all those SAS men I took out,' I joked. There was a split second where I could see him weigh up the likelihood of this remark being true.

In keeping with the IRA's left-wing ethos in the H-blocks, they sought to give roles to as many men as possible to 'give them a sense of ownership of the commune' and to allow them to 'develop within the role'. I always liked the IRA engaging in the touchy-feely language of the 1990s. Often, young and inexperienced volunteers were chosen. Some older men and those of a cynical disposition would dismiss this as 'tokenism'. 'Who did he ever shoot?' cynics asked. But the IRA had a policy of choosing people they considered capable of carrying out the task. It was often a meritocratic call, which I thought was very enlightened. Many of the H-block OCs were in the IRA, some weren't.

There was a little initiation ritual for every new OC. At regular times, lunch (12.30–2 p.m.), tea (4–5 p.m.) and final lock-up each night (8 p.m.), the screws would shout down the wing for us to lock-up. We ignored any such instruction from them and waited on the IRA, in the shape of the OC, to tell us to lock-up, usually a couple of minutes later. The order was usually given in Irish, '*Sin faoi ghlas*'. On the first day of any new OC's stint the lads would create a bit of tension by shouting 'speech, speech' and banging cups on tables. No one ever made a speech, of course. It was just a little fun. As I readied myself to shout the order, Frankie Quinn, from east Tyrone, led the catcalls, table thumping and banter. When the fuss died down, I drew breath: 'As a black man, it gives me great pleasure to order twenty-three white men to lock-up. *Sin faoi ghlas*, lads.' A loud cheer and laughter swept around the canteen.

In previous eras of jail conflict, the OC carried a lot of weight. I wondered if something major might be around the corner: a jail protest, a flare-up with loyalists down on the visits, or some such drama. Would I be party to any orders to escalate a campaign, perhaps? But really I knew any Godfather-style fantasies would never come to pass.

One Sunday, I was approached before mass by one of the lads who told me the priest had asked to speak to the OC. I brought this rather concerned-looking priest into my cell for privacy.

'How can I help you Father?' I asked.

'I need to speak to the IRA,' he replied.

'You've come to the right place,' I joked. He didn't laugh.

'I was asked to see if you could do anything,' he added in a pleading tone. 'A lad from Tyrone has been taken away by some of your men and his family asked me if I could speak to you to get him home safely.' I immediately regretted my flippant attitude. My instinct was to tell him some good news, so that he could give the family hope regarding their son. I knew I wasn't the answer to his prayers, but I knew a man who might be. It just so happened that at that time, H6 was also home to Bobby Storey, an important member of the camp staff and a man of considerable influence within the republican movement. The solution we came up with was as simple as it was honest – I told the priest that while we sympathised with the situation we could do nothing about it because, as prisoners, we had no idea what the IRA was doing on the outside. I conveyed this message in as sympathetic a way as possible to the priest and then listened closely to the news for some days after. I was delighted to find that no one was reported missing and no informers were killed by the IRA in Tyrone or elsewhere.

Notions of leading the men to the barricades melted away as I found myself bogged down in what was essentially light admin work for the IRA. At times it was as if I'd been sent to the H-blocks by a temping agency that had the IRA as a client. I was heading up the IRA's Human Resources department.

I remember many of my fellow prisoners from my days in

H6. Belfast-man Ned Flynn was usually to be found on an exercise bike on the landing with a radio clamped to his ear. He took great pleasure in hearing how badly England were doing in the cricket, 'England's middle order collapsed, Gatting's out, LBW and they may have to follow on,' he shouted to an uncomprehending, uncaring wing.

Mark Cleary was eighteen when he and two friends were in a chip shop after a game of snooker. Purely because they were young Catholics they were attacked by two older loyalists. In the ensuing melee, a loyalist was struck on the head and died. As victims of an unprovoked attack Mark and his friends expected to face manslaughter charges but instead they were charged with murder and received life sentences.

Peter 'Skeet' Hamilton was a throwback to the 1970s. He was part of the 1983 escape but got caught not far from the jail. Running across fields in search of some form of transport as sirens blared in the background, Skeet, spotted a group of twelve comrades running as a group. He decided he was better off going it alone as a large group was bound to be spotted. He saw a farm and thought he could commandeer a vehicle. 'Well, I say farm,' Skeet used to say as we walked the yard, 'Worst fuckin' farm in Ireland. Not only did it not have a car, but the miserable bastards didn't even have a fuckin' horse I could steal.' He was captured close to the jail trying to hold his breath as screws stood on the bank of a river waiting for him to surface.

In a spartanly decorated cell facing my own was Billy Gorman, the marathon man. According to the RUC, Billy shot a policeman in the head at point-blank range even though Billy was, at the time of the killing, a fifteen-year-old schoolboy. Being the fittest man in the jail was a change for Billy as he had previously been known as 'Billy Hotplate', due to his habit of standing by the cooker, making snacks all day. After the 1983 breakout his dad reprimanded him for being so fat that he couldn't run. For Billy, the rest of his long sentence was a regime of careful eating, weight training and running mini marathons around the yard. He trained for freedom while quietly protesting his innocence. Billy spent the best years of his life in jail. After eleven years each lifer would be subject to an annual review to see if he was eligible for release. Year after year Billy was knocked back. On one occasion he came back in from the governor's office after his review meeting.

'How did it go, Billy?' I asked.

'Knocked back,' he said, still smiling.

I grimaced but could think of nothing to say.

'Ah, well,' he said, 'back into the trenches for another year.'

It is hard to believe now – given the IRA's cessation of hostilities in 1994, its decision to decommission its weapons and the coalition government it shares with the Democratic Unionist Party – but in the late 1980s and early 1990s the word 'ceasefire' was anathema to many republicans. Prisoners pored over speeches from British ministers including one from Peter Brooke who, cleverly, spoke to members of the republican movement and their families. He mentioned our quality of life – the long jail terms, the risk of death, the low incomes or trying to survive on the dole. He was making the point that the armed struggle had gone as far as it could and that dialogue was the way forward. Brooke made this point rather eloquently with the antiquated maxim, 'the game is not worth the candle'. In 1992, the movement was on the ropes politically. Gerry Adams lost the West Belfast Westminster seat to the moderate nationalist party the SDLP (Social Democratic and Labour Party) whose candidate, Joe Hendron, had done a deal with the unionists. Although a unionist could not get elected in west Belfast they still had around five thousand votes and could influence the outcome by voting tactically for Hendron. Adams won the seat back in 1997 and has never come close to losing it since.

In 1992, loyalists shot dead five Catholics in a bookmaker's shop in south Belfast. A small detail from an unlikely source struck home that day. RUC Chief Constable Hugh Annesley, flanked by his senior staff, walked up to the cameras at the scene of the attack and prefaced his remarks about the shooting with the phrase: 'This is murder madness.' It helped to crystallise some thoughts that were floating around in my head. The politics of condemnation never worried me much – I certainly didn't think we were in the wrong – but I began to wonder where the struggle was heading.

A bomb in Warrington in 1993 killed two children and injured several innocent people. It was a devastating moment that was milked for all it was worth by the media and our political opponents. The intensity of the conflict contrasted with the tantalising prospect of a cessation of hostilities. It was not the case that the IRA felt they couldn't go on but, I believed, that at some point talks would have to begin, so 1994 seemed as good a time as any. Besides, talks had been going on behind the scenes for years. Much was made in the media of the role of the prisoners on key votes about whether to accept or reject the various moves that the IRA and Sinn Féin leadership proposed. We were billed as the hard men, the uncompromising militants. I was never convinced that we were as important as the media suggested – we often deferred to the people outside as they had a far better idea of what was really going on. In my role as OC, I had a slight thrill in reading out some comms sent in from the Army Council of the IRA. They were invariably tersely worded statements with no fat at all. This was important as such statements would be analysed to death by men looking for hints about amnesties.

I felt guilty about a more immediate selfish interest: if ceasefires were called on all sides then my chances of being shot diminished while the prospects of carving out a career would be enhanced. The idea of being hemmed into west Belfast, possibly doing bar work, filled me with dread and I knew I would have to take risks with my personal safety if I wanted to fulfil my dreams.

In July 1994, weeks before my first parole stint, the IRA killed two loyalists in south Belfast. They were dangerous men and the IRA decided to take them out of the equation before silencing their own weapons. Tensions were running high and, as the likelihood of ceasefire seemed to be slipping away, I was nervous. But along with the bullets, the prospect of hope and real progress also filled the air. In the summer of 1994 the IRA flirted with the British government over terms for a ceasefire. Influential Irish-American businessmen with impressive credentials and influence at the White House, flew in to meet Gerry Adams and other Sinn Féin leaders. My first parole was booked for early August and the ceasefire was called at the end of that month. Our world was changing. Some of us embraced change; some on all sides resisted it.

My permanent release from jail in June 1995 was not the most spectacular day of my life. I had acclimatised on paroles during the final year of my sentence. I noticed while inside that DJs on Radio One referred to their 'website' and some young people were running around with mobile phones. On the other hand, the Tories were still in power. When the day arrived I was keen to keep things low-key as many men still faced long years of incarceration. The solidarity and comradeship forged in jail could never be matched by relationships on the outside. I said my goodbyes, took one last lap of the yard on my own and left.

My time inside was an inspiring, unforgettable experience and in some ways, it deepened me as a person but, like most prisoners, I think I could have done without the inconvenience. Being in jail has helped me maintain a sense of perspective about other issues in my life since my release. I do not see it as wasted time; I am not bitter about it and I do not blame anyone.

My brother Damian and Mum were at the gates when I walked out and we drove straight to a supermarket. 'Timothy, queue up there and get bacon and sausages. Make sure the bacon's not too fatty. Tell the man to give you bacon from the middle in case flies have been on the top slices.' It felt as though I'd never been away.

The Enemy Within

I was buzzing on my release from jail but it was a low-key, private joy. My family and friends were happy, I was happy and that was all that mattered. My younger brother Paddy, who had been my unofficial and unpaid gofer, was probably happiest of all. He had been with me every step of the way, sending in money, clothes and arranging visits for me without complaint. It would take time to adjust to society and the pace of life but to begin with I just wanted to have fun; get drunk, stay out late and live a little. I met up with two girls who used to come to see me in prison. We went to a club and I savoured the pounding dance music, the glitter and sparkle of the girls, the heady atmosphere. This was what I had been missing.

I got work in a bar, mostly working at night, and also began attending a very basic media course called E Force during the day – it was aimed at those who had been on the dole for over a year and I had made inquiries into studying journalism just before I went into jail. Five years later, just weeks after my release, I finally seized the chance to enrol on this course. I felt it was important to try and make a career for myself despite the obstacles my past would create.

While recording vox pops in the city centre one morning with a friend from the course, a guy in a baseball cap came up to me and said, 'Brannigan?' After a few seconds I realised that he was a loyalist ex-prisoner. He smirked and stared but walked on. Some weeks later in a dark, empty backstreet another guy kept staring at me. I thought nothing of it but after a few more steps I turned around to check if he was still there and he had struck what, presumably, he thought was a menacing pose. He stood motionless, his arm fully stretched and his index finger pointing right at me. It was almost as if he had an imaginary rifle in his hand. I laughed to myself and walked on. Posers like that were not the people I had to worry about. If I was going to be shot, I probably wouldn't even hear them coming, I figured.

The key point of the course was that we got placements in local media outlets. It might be with a small radio station or a local newspaper but it was still a foot in the door. I couldn't believe my luck when the course organiser told us that the local arm of GMTV was looking for a trainee reporter. We were encouraged to go for interviews the following day. I decided to wear a shirt, tie and blazer while others went casually dressed. I was politically aware so their questions about local politicians and political parties weren't a problem and I was given the post. I didn't tell them about my recent spell in prison.

Within months of leaving jail I was reporting on local news for GMTV. I worked normal office hours, getting interviews, pictures and quotes on tape, but I didn't appear on TV. After a month or so, I was urged to record actual reports but I thought that if I appeared on screen the RUC, loyalists, prison officers or any number of other groups would recognise me as having been inside and my cover would be blown. Therefore I actively avoided appearing on screen.

In February 1996 the IRA detonated a massive bomb at Canary Wharf in London in what the media liked to dub a 'spectacular'. The IRA saw London as a prestige target and big bombs would generate considerable propaganda. The Canary Wharf bomb went off on Friday night and, on the Sunday afterwards, I was told to do a report. I had to record a piece to camera at Belfast City Hall telling viewers that 'Later today thousands of trade unionists will gather here at the City Hall to demand that the ceasefire be reinstated. This is Tim Brannigan,

GMTV, at Belfast City Hall.' We did several nervy takes. I wasn't nervous of the camera so much as being the centre of any controversy the following day. I thought of the potential for angry phone calls:

'What's that Provie bastard doing on my TV?' or perhaps: 'Do you know your reporter's just out of the H-blocks and did time for weapons and explosives?'

Another take was recorded and used across four bulletins the next morning. When I went to work at 9 a.m. on the Monday I expected to be asked to leave. I assumed that some people had rung the office. In my blazer pocket I had a short, grateful letter of thanks and resignation for my bosses, Barbara McCann and Patricia Wilkinson, both of whom read the bulletins in the mornings. But nothing was said. As the day wore on I began to consider the significance of the moment. I was, perhaps, the first former republican prisoner ever to report on an IRA bomb on the TV news. I soon heard that some of the lads in the H-blocks thought the situation was hilarious and that others on the Falls thought it was fantastic.

I realised too that with a suit and tie, a microphone and a cameraman for company, people didn't see me as an ex-prisoner. The idea simply never occurred to them. Because this was the era of 'talks about talks' leading up to the Good Friday Agreement, I spent long days at Stormont sitting among the press corps. Rubbing shoulders with these reporters increased my confidence about how to act at press conferences and how to chase stories. I regretted not being able to make more of my opportunity and make more TV appearances. They were certainly offered to me. I was even sounded out for a post in London, which would have been brilliant, but deep down I knew that any success with GMTV would be short-lived, as my story would be exposed eventually. Going to the office with resignation letters already written and fearing success in my job was no way to work.

In 1997 I got the chance to make a short documentary as part of a series for Channel 4. They were looking for tales of the 'black diaspora'. We made a short film comparing the experience of being black in the very white city of Belfast and being black in the multi-racial city of Liverpool. I got to present the show but made sure to describe myself as a nationalist, not a republican. We filmed in west Belfast with republican murals as a backdrop and we also filmed in Liverpool where the most salient point to be made was that Liverpool was, sadly, quite a segregated city racially. The documentary and my GMTV experience helped secure a place on a postgraduate diploma in journalism and in 1998 I was chosen to do a placement in the features section of a local paper.

The *Irish News* is the regional morning paper in Northern Ireland. Its readership then was almost exclusively nationalist, Catholic and, in the main, middle-aged. People bought it to study the horses, read death notices and to follow the latest Troubles or Peace Process events. The paper was ignored by many young people and, in particular, young women who favoured tabloids, glossy magazines and the internet. I was relieved to be working mostly in features although I sometimes had to do news stories. Working on the newsdesk would have meant dealing with the police and going to events that I might have found problematic. It could be dangerous enough being identified as an *Irish News* reporter, without carrying the baggage I had. Indeed, I was asked to attend the funeral of a UVF paramilitary killed by his own bomb but luckily I had booked the day off so someone else had to go.

On several occasions, I covered stories in loyalist areas including the discovery of a girl's body in a coal shed in the lower Shankill area. I once covered a story for GMTV in a loyalist estate. Not even the cameraman I was with was aware of the pressure I was under; nor was he aware of my back-ground. I was worried some loyalist ex-prisoner would spot me. Luckily I managed to remain anonymous. The *Irish News* didn't know about my jail time. I thought they might not give me work if they did and, besides, I didn't feel that I should spend the rest of my life apologising for my past.

I was also given the difficult task of covering the shooting of Andy Kearney from west Belfast. He had been in a row with an alleged IRA commander in a bar. Their dispute escalated and Kearney was later shot in the legs in a block of flats and bled to death. The Kearney shooting presented difficulties for me. It was being described as a 'murder' and the IRA was being blamed. I wouldn't normally use the word 'murder' in relation to the IRA and my story mentioned a man being 'killed' but I knew that the news editor would change this to 'murdered'. I decided to go and see Sinn Féin, explaining my views on the terminology. I also told them that, in future, I would not be explaining myself to them after every story. They understood perfectly and were more pleased that I had been able to get some work. Wondering how other people would react was a heavy burden. I suppose I always knew that things would come to a head and that my time in prison would come out.

The *Irish News* rang me just as my course came to an end and asked if I was free to work three days a week filling the entertainment section, Metro. I jumped at the chance to write about music and movies and not having to worry about controversial news stories. The entertainment guide, which appeared every Friday, was a bit dull. It was supposed to be aimed at young people but featured country and western music, folk singers and even long articles on choral society concerts. Luckily, my line manager was of the view that things had to change. I could not have arrived at a better time.

I had no particular background in celebrity journalism but I did bring enthusiasm and energy to the task. My passion for the job came across in the articles I wrote, which were mainly directed at my target audience of eighteen- to thirty-five-year-olds, although judging by the reactions and mail I received the audience went well beyond that group. One early article discussed the names some young couples and young mums gave their children. It seemed to cause a stir as I made the point that our own Irish heritage and many centuries of beautiful names were being marginalised in favour of names like Kylie,

Britney, Courtney, and Chloe. Around the same time, some observations on the seeming inability of a generation of young women in Belfast to wear properly fitting bras got a positive reaction from female readers. I was soon given my own column, comprising *Sex and the City* style features with humorous tales about Belfast's nightlife, youth culture and my own personal 'man about town' misadventures. I started to get regular interviews with proper celebrities including Emma Bunton, Destiny's Child and Rod Stewart and would deliberately mention A-listers in articles to justify putting glamorous photographs of celebrities into the paper. In targeting young readers, I approached companies such as Tommy Hilfiger, Gap, Next and Calvin Klein for free gifts in competitions. The paper's market research vindicated my approach and the management made it clear they wanted to change the paper's grey image.

In December 1998 I applied for and got a permanent job at the *Irish News*. I remember that at around the same time I heard a line from, of all people, David Trimble, the Ulster Unionist Party leader and Northern Ireland's First Minister. He said, 'Just because you have a past, doesn't mean you can't have a future.' It was a comment aimed squarely at people such as me and I felt elated when I heard it.

In the year 2000 I won Newcomer of the Year at the Institute of Public Relations journalism awards. It was especially significant for me given that I'd been in jail. It was official recognition. I rang Mum.

'I won! I won, Mum!'

'Oh, love, I can't believe it. I really can't.'

'Hope you're proud of me. This is for you.'

'I am, love. I am.'

My relationship with Mum had become quite settled. I had moved out and was living in my own place – a shoebox of a flat in a sprawling working-class estate – and this had improved our relationship. At one family function she sat with some relatives and, after years of hearing her siblings talk proudly about the achievements of their children, took great delight in getting me to talk about my job. 'Timothy, who was that singer you met? Not Myleene, the other one. Was it Britney or Beyoncé?' she asked before sitting back to savour the moment as I told tales of meeting glamorous pop stars. People stopped her in the street to tell her how pleased they were that I had got such a good job after being in jail. Mum was extremely proud.

When I called down to Mum's for Sunday dinner things were calm and relaxed. At one dinner she asked me if I'd noticed anything different about her. I looked at the colour of her hair, its length, her roots. I examined her glasses too but could see nothing different. 'What is it Mum? I give up.'

'I'm on Prozac!' she said.

I didn't know much about Prozac other than that it attracted the label 'wonder drug', but I was all for anything that had Mum in a good mood. She had been close to breakdown at several points in her life, including after my arrest. She coped with these moments in various ways but prescription drugs had long been part of her armoury.

Mum and I got on extremely well during this period. We met up in town some Saturdays. If I timed it right, I could head to a select number of shops and track her down even without prearranging it. Marks & Spencer's food hall on a Saturday afternoon around five was always a sure bet. We had coffee in various cafes, especially those that overlooked the busy streets as we both enjoyed people watching. We had serious conversations and she urged me to go and work for a 'big magazine in London'. She also wanted me to travel and not settle for Belfast no matter how well things were going. Mum had bigger dreams than any of us.

At this stage though, Belfast was doing just fine by me. I was working for the *Irish News*, writing for my own community. And then, one Thursday afternoon in the year 2000, the phone call that I had been dreading finally came. 'Is that Tim Brannigan?'

'Yes.'

'This is Martin O'Hagan at the *Sunday World*. Do you mind if I ask you a question?'

'Go on,' I said, getting anxious.

'Tim, were you inside?'

'What are you talking about?'

'Look, Tim. I know all about you and I've been inside, too. I'm trying to help you here.'

'How are you trying to help?'

'The *Sunday Mirror* is going to try and bury you this weekend,' he said. My heart missed several beats – all the noise and chatter of the newsroom disappeared.

'They might call you today. A reporter has got your details and now he wants to expose you.' The journalist was married to a cop, I was told.

Martin O'Hagan was not a republican by any means. He had built a career as a journalist with a reputation for uncovering the gangsterism and drug dealing at the heart of the loyalist paramilitary groups. While some dismiss the *Sunday World* as dealing in scandal, sleaze and sex, it has put many other papers to shame in terms of the number of exposés and exclusives it has uncovered.

I was shattered by the imminent story. Martin said that he knew the journalist working on the story well and would try to persuade him not to run it. I feared that I was about to be exposed in a sensational way and that I would lose my job. The management at the *Irish News* still didn't know that not only was I a republican but one who had a conviction and was not very long out of the H-blocks. I had never lied to the *Irish News*, I just hadn't volunteered the information.

I could only hope that my track record at the paper would stand me in good stead. I had no option but to go to the management at the newspaper and tell them about my stint in prison. They were surprised when I told them I had been in the H-blocks but their reaction was much more positive than I had expected. Firstly, they reassured me that my job was safe, they then said that they would get in touch with the *Sunday Mirror*. They were willing to go on the offensive and fight on my behalf. It was a difficult situation and they handled it well. The story was dropped after several interventions from various people within the Mirror Group, the National Union of Journalists and the *Irish News*. My secret was out. Waves of relief washed over me for some time afterwards. I thanked Martin for stepping in, even though he didn't know me. When I saw him in a bar sometime later, he wouldn't even accept a thank-you drink.

Even though I didn't have to conceal my past any more, my status as an ex-prisoner continued to make me a target. I remember being stopped by the police one day as I headed back to the office with a colleague. My friend asked the cop why he was being questioned. 'Because you're with him,' the RUC man replied, nodding in my direction.

I also continued to have serious concerns for my safety. My profile and photograph appeared regularly in the *Irish News* and it made me feel vulnerable. Loyalists knew where I worked and if they wanted they could easily get me going to the office or heading home. Some journalists said I was overreacting – they confidently predicted that a journalist wouldn't be murdered.

On 28 September 2001, the year after he had helped me, Martin O'Hagan was shot dead by loyalists as he walked near his home with his wife.

Peggy's Not Well

On the evening of 19 October 2002 I was planning my Saturday night out and had just collected a Chinese take-away when Chris rang me on my mobile. 'It's your mum,' he said. 'She's not well.'

'What's wrong?'

'She was getting ready to go into town this afternoon when she found she couldn't move her right arm and that one side of her face felt funny. She says she'll be all right and won't let me call a doctor.'

'Jesus Christ, Chris, she's had a stroke!' I said. Chris had nursed her all day but she was adamant that she was fine and that it would pass. I told Chris that I was on my way over and that we needed to get her to hospital. I was surprised that she was so insistent on not getting medical attention given that she was often at the GP surgery. I realised later that she must have been very frightened.

When I got to the house, Mum was agitated and I immediately announced that she was going to hospital. She was defiant and her tone was one I'd known all my life: anger that would tolerate no challenge to her authority. But now, I was much surer of my ground when arguing with Mum. I knew when to back off and when to pursue a point. The stroke had greatly impaired her speech and, most alarmingly for me, her memory was significantly affected. During the day, while ill, she had been trying to remember our names and the names of her brothers. My concern was that the wasted hours might have led to lasting damage. I was angry with Chris but as someone who had bowed to Mum's will more times than I cared to remember, I didn't say anything. I was firm about how things should be handled in future. 'Next time anything like this happens, call me and get an ambulance, no matter what she says and no matter how angry she seems.' Mum was mumbling half-garbled sentences but her tone was un-mistakably irate. I spoke to her clearly and calmly but told her she wasn't well and that she had to go to the hospital to get better. She was worried that she didn't look her best and that she had no make-up on. We finally escorted her, complaining, to the car and drove to the Royal Victoria Hospital.

It was our misfortune that Mum was ill on a weekend night. Staff were stretched to breaking point. Getting to see a con-sultant or even a junior doctor took hours. I knew that people could bounce back from strokes and that all was not lost but it was hard to stay positive as I watched Mum drawing on oxygen and pointing while mumbling nonsensical words or silently mouthing names. She was struggling to remember who among us were her sons and who were her brothers.

I had contacted my brothers and aunts and uncles. There was nothing we could do and a large group of us milled around in the waiting area. Every time a nurse or the duty doctor came to us with news, we uttered the same mantra, 'That's good. She's in good hands. There's no better place for her to be. They know what they're doing.'

Luckily, Mum made a quick and almost full recovery. A few of us were in the room with her when a registrar came in. He spoke vaguely about tests and told us that we would have to wait and see. Initial scans had shown a 'shadow' or 'dark area' on her brain, the doctor told us, 'but apart from that' every-thing 'seemed' normal. It could be nothing, he said. What does 'apart from that' mean or 'seemed' normal, I thought. These qualifying phrases didn't reassure me. I'd had too many consultations with lawyers to put too much store by the modifying words they used. Mum, on the other hand, focused on the word 'normal'. Before he left the room he repeated a significant sentence, 'So, as I say, it all seems normal except for that little shadow … whatever it is …' I could see he was trying to find a way to end the sentence as Mum, by now oblivious, thanked him and all of his staff. 'So, we'll keep a wee eye on that and see how it goes …'

We all gave Mum a hug. 'From now on there'll be lots of hugs and lots of kisses,' she said euphorically. Although Mum seemed happy, I knew that we were probably not out of the woods yet. Her speech did bounce back to about ninety or even ninety-five per cent of what it had been but this was only a temporary reprieve. Within days, the slight stammering in her speech, confusion about names and some reduction in the freedom of her movements set in again.

As 2002 came to a close, everything else seemed to be going well. I was still attracting reasonable celebrities to the paper and was pleased that the feedback appeared very positive. I was also settling into a new house that I'd bought in Beechmount, a few minutes from the family home. As the only son not married with a family of his own, I never missed a Christmas dinner at home. But that year as we ate my brother Damien and I swapped concerned glances as Mum struggled with her speech.

Mum was due to turn seventy on 15 January 2003. I booked a venue and a cabaret act who sang Doris Day, Frank Sinatra and Dean Martin songs. We decorated the room with balloons and I got some posters printed on *Irish News* branded sheets used at newspaper kiosks that thunder out the top headline of the day: 'Marks & Spencer's shares slump as Peggy stops shopping'. We tracked down some of Mum's old friends, including a man who had asked her out several times as a teenager. Her brothers and sisters came, as did many of her friends. I told her that I was bringing her and Chris to a nice restaurant for a meal. 'Isn't this place lovely? Oh look, a winding staircase. Beautiful,' she said as we walked up the stairs. She was a veteran in making appreciative noises when someone was being nice to her. I hung back a step or two and when she got near the top the silence of the waiting crowd broke to cheers of 'Happy birthday, Peggy!' 'I'll kill you,' she joked, before going on to have what she described as 'the best night of my life'.

The dancing, drinking, laughing and her decision to tell several people her story and the details of my birth made it a tiring night and her speech was badly affected the next day. I told her to rest but she was eager to relive every minute of it. The world was about to change dramatically for Mum and the worst twenty-four-hour period of my life was about to begin.

'This is what will take you away, Margaret'

The week after Mum's birthday I decided to take some time off to use up annual leave and decorate my new house. A friend, Aeneas, also a reporter at the *Irish News*, called to my home one evening and, as we chatted, the phone rang. Chris told me that Mum was ill again and that they would pick me up on the way to the hospital.

When I saw Mum it was clear that she had had another stroke. Her speech was garbled but her tone was unmistakeably angry. Chris and I knew that she didn't want to go to hospital. She was confused and scared. I kept repeating firmly that she would be home again soon but that she had to go to the hospital and that was the end of the matter.

As the doctors attended to Mum on a trolley, I contacted my brothers. We stood around awaiting news and then agreed that since I was off that week I would stay as everyone else had to get up for work the next day. They found Mum a bed on a general ward and I pulled the faded floral curtain around us for privacy. Mum lay motionless. The lights were dimmed and only one, above her bed, shed a small pool of light around us. The air felt cool and I covered her up with a blanket. I asked her to squeeze my hand if she could hear me. I was certain that there might be a hint of recognition but there was nothing. I rested my arm alongside hers. Mum's skin felt a bit cool, waxy almost, and I could see that her eyebrows were shapeless and the little wrinkles around her mouth seemed more pronounced than before. For the first time, Mum looked her age; it was quite a shock.

I thought about the struggles she had endured in her life. I knew that she'd experienced enormous pressures and that she had kept her dignity and fought for what she believed to be right. Time drifted by. I sat back in the hard plastic chair and hoped for a little sleep. I closed my eyes but as I did so an almighty scream from Mum made me jump. I looked up and it seemed as if someone was pushing Mum into the bed. Her eyes were as wide as possible and were fixed on the ceiling.

Within seconds there were five or six medical staff around her bed. Medical staff gave each other orders but I could sense that they were in the dark to some extent as Mum had only been on the ward a matter of hours and was still being assessed. After about ten minutes and several more screams, a nurse ran to the supplies room. I stepped forward. 'Is she going to survive, nurse?' I asked.

'Are you a relative?'

'Her son. She was just sleeping and then this almighty scream came out,' I said. 'It seems bad. Perhaps I should phone my relatives?'

'It might be worth telling them to come,' she said. 'Is she religious? You might want to get the priest. I can arrange that for you,' she added in a low, kind voice.

I feared that if I went down the corridor to make some calls she might die. I didn't want her to die alone. I called the family at about 4 a.m and soon they were at her bedside. The priest arrived and gave Mum the Last Rites. Frantic minutes gave way to hours and, as daylight crept in, Mum was still fighting. She fought back day by day, slowly regaining some strength and movement.

The consultant told us that the test results had revealed a glioblastoma, an aggressive tumour on the left-hand side of her brain near her ear. He told us about the risks of surgery and the chances of buying some time. He was choosing his words carefully. I was frightened and began to cry as I heard the doctor tiptoe around the hard facts and try to accentuate the positive. In truth, only Mum could see any good news. The rest of us merely pretended and I was annoyed that our faces betrayed our real thoughts and fears. Mum saw our distress and bit her bottom lip. 'It's not me I'm worried about, it's them,' she said to the doctor. She was discharged and we left the Royal by the Falls Road entrance and went out to the cars. Mum and I were last out of the lift and moved slowly as the others walked ahead chatting. 'So, Mum,' I asked, 'how do you feel after that?'

'Well, at least he didn't mention cancer,' she said as we began to cross the road.

'Ach Mum,' I said before stopping myself. Clearly she had not understood the meaning of glioblastoma.

Mum was scheduled to have an operation to remove the tumour – we were told that this might give her another three months to live. All of us were in the hospital when she was wheeled down the corridor and into the surgery. She waved with both hands and blew kisses in an obvious attempt to convince us that this was no big deal.

After the operation, I attended meetings with Mum where different doctors and consultants told her that while the operation had been successful and would extend her life, she was going to die. As the doctors spoke in clinical terms about her condition Mum nodded and said 'Uh-huh' at the end of some of their sentences, but I could see she didn't always fully understand what was being said to her. After a short course of radiotherapy to control the growth of the tumour in April and May 2003 a consultant told her, 'There's no more that we can do.' Mum understood this to mean that there was no more that *needed* to be done and that she had been cured. She took us all out to an upmarket restaurant in Belfast for dinner. Our cousin worked there as manager and organised a bottle of champagne to celebrate Mum's 'good news'. We all played along, as it was great to see her happy.

Another doctor told her 'This is what will take you away, Margaret.' 'Gee-whiz,' Mum replied. She often said 'Gee-whiz' to express mild surprise or bemusement. It seemed the epitome of understatement. She looked at me. I didn't speak because I knew I would go to pieces. It was one of the defining moments of my life.

I went over to Mum's house one afternoon to see how she was doing. At this stage, she was fine to be left alone, but she was becoming increasingly dependent on the family. I walked into the kitchen. Mum often washed her hair at the kitchen sink. She was bent over with her head below the mixer tap. Her hair was heavily lathered in white soapy bubbles but instead of her usual vigorous rinsing she was totally still. I ran over and asked if she was all right. I tested the temperature of the water. It was quite cool so I added some more warm water and then began rinsing her hair. 'I used to be able to do this myself, love,' she said.

'I know, but it's no problem, I'm a hairdresser, remember? Remember you got me the job and wrote the lovely letter?' She could not see that I was filling up.

'Oh aye, that's right.'

My brothers, Chris and myself wanted Mum to be cared for at home and I could tell that she wouldn't be able to be left alone for much longer. So, in May 2003 I resigned from the *Irish News* to look after her full-time. Chris would leave for work before 7 a.m. and I would try to make it up to Mum's house before she woke. I would spend the day with her. For several months she still had the strength to go into town and we followed a familiar routine of TK Maxx, Tesco and Marks & Spencer. In spite of her increasing frailty and confusion I resisted wrapping Mum in cotton wool, so if she wanted to shop we did just that. Mostly she didn't need anything and was happy to experience the familiar sights and sounds of the town. I viewed this as therapy for her and I was pleased with the level of care we, as a family, provided for her.

When I took her out and about Mum would try to tell friends that she was mostly well. She would speak a language of half words in the wrong order but recognisable phrases and coherent short sentences came out too. One afternoon, in Marks & Spencer, an old woman from the Shankill Road tapped Mum on the shoulder. 'Peggy?' Mum's face lit up. The two women chatted and Mum tried to tell the woman her story. I always allowed Mum to say things on her own even if they were almost unintelligible. Her hand touched her heart and then she dragged the palm of her hand across her stomach. 'Says, fine, fine, fine. Always fine. Just this…' She pointed to her head. 'Surgeon man says, "No, no, no. I make you better. Home." Better, better, better.' This was Mum's attempt to tell her friend that the doctors had told her that all of her major organs were fine and that she had always been in great health but unfortunately this little lump had come.

As we walked around town I was concerned about Mum's balance and worried that I was making her walk too quickly. I asked her to hold my hand so she could lead and set the pace. She liked this and sometimes I would squeeze her hand or she would squeeze mine just for the sake of it. We soon noticed that people stared at us when we held hands. We saw women nudge each other and nod in our direction. Some would be laughing or smirking and they clearly thought I was Mum's toy boy. Mum was delighted that people thought she was walking around town with her six-feet-tall black lover. 'Wouldn't be the first time, Mum.' She looked at me, raised her eyebrows and smiled in a knowing, slightly guilty way.

Chris did much of the caring in the evenings when he got home from work although Mum, exhausted by her trips to town and hospital, usually sat in her chair then went to bed early. One morning, exhausted, I slept in. Mum, a few streets away, sensed an imminent stroke and got out of bed. She slid down the stairs and managed to open the front door. Women leaving their children to the primary school beside our house saw her in her nightdress trying to summon help. I got a call from Paddy and immediately raced to Mum. I promised I'd never leave her vulnerable again.

Once more Mum ended up in hospital. She was given steroids intravenously but the dosage was a bit high and she became hysterical with pain. A nurse from west Belfast spent almost her entire shift with Mum crying and wailing in her arms as the drugs took hours to leave her body. 'There, there, Margaret. I know, I know. Oh, it's terrible but you're going to be all right, love. You'll soon be going home to your own house,' the nurse repeated in a calming whisper.

Mum's deteriorating speech indicated that the tumour was getting bigger. Epileptic fits became a possibility too. Our only option was a second operation. We knew that this carried with it the risk that surgeons could cut away good tissue as well as the tumour and we balanced buying more time against the impact of serious invasive surgery.

The operation went ahead in the summer of 2003. When she returned home, the primary point of contact for Mum was a nurse called Irene O'Neill, a jovial country woman who, like me, thought it better to be positive and matter of fact about Mum's condition. 'How's my wee angel?' Irene would exclaim, popping her head around the door before breezing into our living room like the next hour was going to be the highlight of her day's work, 'How's my favourite patient?' In the beginning Mum had been too proud to let nurses and care assistants into the house. It seemed to her to be an admission that she wasn't well and, possibly worse from Mum's perspective, an indication that she had become an old woman.

I had set up Mum's phone so that my mobile number was the first of the quick dial buttons. I told her not to leave the house and if she wanted anything just to push the button and I would be there. She sometimes looked at her phone like she was seeing it for the first time. On a cold autumn afternoon I was passing McDonald's in town when my mobile went off. I answered to hear Mum sobbing heavily.

'What's wrong, Mum? What's wrong?'

'Hello? Who are you? Are you for me?'

'Mum, it's me, Timothy.'

'Are you my baby?' She cried again.

'Yes. It's me. Tim.'

'Did I get my medicine?'

'Yes and you get more at 5 o'clock but I'll be home before that.'

'You're sure, love?'

'Yes. Don't cry, just have a wee sleep. Do you need anything?'

'I don't know.'

'Well, I'll get potatoes out of Marksies and some things from Tesco for you. I think we need a loaf.'

'Aye, that's good. Will you check the numbers, love?'

She meant check the date on the bread and milk. Bread had to be four days ahead of whatever date it was bought on; five days for milk. By the end of the call, I was in a doorway, trying to catch my breath, trying to stay composed. I found the term 'Are you my baby?' extremely poignant. It made me feel very happy but the fact that she was so confused unsettled me.

I was lucky to have as much time with Mum in her final year as I did and I wanted to make the most of it. We spoke about life and family matters, politics and the future. I asked Mum about her favourite songs and her favourite films. We both liked the film *Butch Cassidy and the Sundance Kid*. I told her it reminded me of being a boy and that the song 'Raindrops Keep Fallin' on My Head' had been a secret favourite of mine since childhood. 'Me too,' she said, 'but doesn't it make you feel a little sad?'

'Yes, and sometimes that's a good thing.'

We spoke about my father and she asked if I would promise to track him down and I said I would. She thought that he was probably in London. I never really liked discussing him but I knew she wanted to have this conversation. She went upstairs and dug around in some drawers and old handbags where she kept old photos and documents. She came down with an envelope and handed it to me. It contained the letters my father had written to her. I read through the thin blue paper. No letter was more than a page long; they were notes more than letters and they all demanded that she meet up with him at various prearranged points. The letters were addressed to her at her home address. It is a determined – or desperate – man who writes such letters to a married woman. One of Michael's notes asked her to 'please, please' meet him outside the Broadway cinema at 7 p.m. Another was dated 1972, six years after I was born. 'He seems keen to meet you, if nothing else, Mum. Why did he want to meet up on all of these various dates?'

'Why do you think?' Mum replied. 'Sometimes men are only after one thing. I went to meet him once to talk about you and your needs and he just wanted other things.'

Of all of the caring that went on nothing affected me more than feeding Mum. As time went on, her appetite diminished. I tried to encourage her to eat. I gave her what people in Belfast call 'potato dinners' – meat and two veg with a bit of gravy. Mum sometimes ate in the kitchen but loved to watch the news while eating so more often she had her food in the living room. One evening I noticed that she could hardly hold her knife and fork. I cut the food up for her and then realised that the only way she was going to eat was if I fed her. I found myself encouraging her as she chewed silently, 'That's brilliant. Look at that clean plate. Hardly any left … Just this last wee bit. Aren't you the good girl? Had enough?'

'Uh-huh,' she would reply.

She had long since given up on having control of the remote although I was sure to keep the news on as she would have done every night. I could see she was now struggling to follow what was happening. She leaned to one side to see over my shoulder as I fed her dinner to her. Tony Blair was on TV. 'Pig!' she said, with a little flicker of her old defiance.

I was exhausted as Christmas 2003 approached. Mum was still determined to look for bargains and presents. On Christmas Eve we went to town and I held her hand as she wandered around the shops. We didn't buy much but it felt right and I was glad that, despite the cold weather, she still wanted to go out. She tried on a hat at a full-length mirror and, as she attempted to get a closer look, she lost her balance and stumbled. She gave herself a fright and I took her home.

As I had never cooked a Christmas dinner, Chris and I decided the sensible thing would be to have dinner at the Ramada Hotel in Belfast on Christmas Day. Mum put on her tweed suit and stumbled around the place making sure everyone could see her. It was sad seeing her struggle with a knife and fork and she didn't notice that some of the food was a bit cold. It was her last day out – she never left the house again.

That Mum had an impact on all who met her, even in her illness, was confirmed for me while I was doing research for this book. In 2008, I was allowed access to her medical records. There were pages of notes and forms in pastel pink, green and yellow discussing procedures and options, diagnoses and prognoses. There were typed requests for scans and handwritten notes and assessments. Placed in chronological order it was easy to see Mum's decline. Then I spotted a handwritten comment from a surgeon to a fellow consultant. It said, 'Thank you for introducing me to this lovely woman. Please let me know how she gets on.' Another note was a summary of a meeting between Mum, the consultant and me. The doctor noted Mum's difficulty in speaking but added that 'her son is able to communicate on her behalf very effectively'.

In early 2004, as Mum deteriorated, we spoke to her GP and Irene and it was decided that we would put a hospital bed in the living room so that we could monitor her constantly. I remember coming home one day to find that a relative had closed the living room curtains and that people in the room were speaking in whispers as Mum lay sleeping. I opened the blinds, turned on the TV and made it clear that Mum's wake would not be starting just yet. I put a CD player in the room and played Dean Martin, Frank Sinatra and Doris Day. Mum loved life and living; I felt this approach was in keeping with her spirit.

As Mum's health declined, the amount of visits from health

and social workers grew until, in the last few months, hardly a day went by that someone didn't call, usually between ten in the morning and lunchtime. The rest of the time, Chris and I looked after Mum. When he got home from work, I updated Chris about the events of the day and explained the ever-changing regime of medicines we had to give Mum. He would update me in the morning and I would take over when Chris headed out to work. My brothers helped when they could. The intimacy of feeding and washing my own mother was not lost on me and I was mindful of how much she'd fought for me. I wanted to make sure we got every detail right and I think we more or less did.

Despite being skint and tired, I decided to join close friend Paul and his girlfriend Ciara for a few Saturday night drinks. It was nice to have a break and the beer and coloured lights had the desired effect. I noticed two girls dancing close to where we sat. They were having fun and I made a little eye contact. Towards the end of the night one of the two dancing girls was making her way past me. I told her that if we were going to go out, she'd have to lose the white trousers she was wearing as they were dreadful. This was clearly a risky conversation starter but it worked because she laughed and we ended up going out. Her name was Nicola. While my circumstances weren't ideal, I did feel that it would be good for me to have something positive in my life to focus on.

Nicola was an art teacher with a real passion for her subject. Her family was from north Belfast and was quite middle class. I knew they were middle class the minute I walked into their their living room because it was possible to walk *around* their furniture. Sofas, chairs and other items stood free in the ample space. In our own house, we sometimes kept the vacuum cleaner, lots of old shoes and, occasionally automatic weapons or bags of gelignite behind the sofa.

I would leave our family home each evening, sometimes to go to my own home, sometimes to Nicola's arms. It was good to have someone to lean on and occasionally let off steam. She would ask how things were and I told her sometimes in detail and sometimes with anger if I was frustrated. I was exhausted but I knew I had to keep going.

On Wednesday 10 March Nicola called me up and said that she wanted to treat me to dinner in a nice restaurant. We went to a place in south Belfast and afterwards drove to her home. No sooner had we arrived in her living room than Damien rang me to say that I should return home as Mum's breathing was very laboured. He agreed to come and collect me. As we walked into the hall Chris was coming down the stairs. 'She's gone,' he said.

Paddy told me that he and Paul had each held a hand as she drew her last breaths. I was pleased that she had died in her own home with her sons there to comfort her. I did not worry about not being there when she died. In fact, I was glad that I was not there to witness it. I leaned over her bed and kissed her forehead.

Closer Than You Think

The eighteen months following Mum's death were difficult for me. In 2006 I went back to doing freelance journalism where I could, but it was only in 2007 that I got up the courage to go in a new direction. I was struck by the increasing number of immigrants coming to live in Northern Ireland from Eastern Europe, Africa and the Philippines. I wasn't the only one to notice their arrival. In some parts of Northern Ireland – mostly but not exclusively Protestant areas – blacks, Asians and Eastern Europeans were being subjected to racial abuse, physical assaults and petrol bomb attacks on their homes and property. These expressions of prejudice were not confined to working-class areas. A spokesman for the Northern Ireland tourism and hospitality sector said that immigrants employed in local hotels and restaurants were 'diluting the brand'. I felt that I could do something better than the local news reports that frequently repeated the glib, unsubstantiated line from German magazine *Der Spiegel* that Northern Ireland was the 'race-hate capital of Europe'. One local TV documentary got a black guy to stand in the centre of a town in Northern Ireland as the bars and clubs emptied out on a Saturday night. They wanted to see if he got attacked for being black. He didn't. I'm not at all sure what point, if any, the programme was trying to make but the presenter seemed to suggest that racism was a small isolated problem caused by a handful of bigots. It was a lazy, complacent conclusion.

I decided to send some programme ideas to producer Tony Phillips at BBC Radio 4 in London. I had met him at a course that gave advice on finding work in radio that had been held in Belfast in the spring of 2006. He seemed impressed by my ideas and called me for a chat. He was curious as to why I'd said that I was well placed to comment on the issue of race in Northern Ireland and we started to discuss my own personal background. He was fascinated by my story. 'Have you ever met your father?' he asked me unexpectedly.

'No.'

'Do you know if he's still alive?'

'I've no idea, to be honest.'

'Are you going to try and find him?'

'I've no plans to at the moment although I did make a promise to my mum that I would do it at some stage.'

'Well, how about we make a programme about your search for your father.'

'Really? Wow!'

'Look, I think this could be a fantastic story and if he's still alive I think we might be able to take you to meet him wherever he is, whether it's London or Africa.'

And with that discussion, my life was given renewed purpose. I felt energised and excited but I also felt a little bit nervous about who my father was, what he would be like, and how he would react to me. What would he think when his love child stepped out of the shadows after forty years?

When I decided to search for my father I went to see a woman called Maggie, who worked for the Family Care Society. Her job was to liaise with people who had been adopted when they wanted to try and trace their families. She gave me this warning: 'If you don't want to hurt anyone we should end this meeting now and you should go home.' I pretended to take her comment on board but in truth I felt it was a little excessive. Documenting my quest for my father in a programme for Radio 4 seemed like too good an opportunity to turn down. The project would allow me to practise radio journalism while also giving me a great chance to find my father. The project involved serious personal issues for me, but I also had to treat it professionally and think about how it would inform and entertain an audience of middle-class, mostly English radio listeners. I started keeping a radio diary. It might be good, I thought, if my research ran into a few dead ends, if I rang lots of numbers and got nowhere before discovering a box of documents which would lead to a shocking revelation. But the actual search didn't take months and it didn't involve wrong turns or weeks of searching library basements. The reason for this was due entirely to my mum's foresight forty years previously. The first bit of good fortune came as a result of her decision to give me my father's surname as my middle name. Now, after decades of feeling slightly self-conscious and ambivalent about the name Ekue, it proved to be the key that opened doors to a new world. All I had to do was visit the General Register Office in central Belfast and type the name into a computer. But I hesitated. What might I find when I embarked on this journey? How would I feel if I discovered my father was dead and that I'd left it too late to begin the search? How would I feel if he was still alive? What if he didn't want to meet me? What if I didn't like him? What if I did like him?

I entered the General Register Office in central Belfast that held records on births, deaths and marriages on people born in Northern Ireland. There couldn't be many people in Belfast born with the name Ekue. Five results came up. I couldn't believe it. Then I realised what was happening. These five names were all registered between 1958 and 1970. They were the children of Mr Michael Ekue and his wife.

I had just discovered five new brothers and sisters. Sisters! I didn't have a sister and now I had three of them. The addresses given suggested a migration across south Belfast with the later children being born after the family had moved from the Ravenhill Road to the more affluent Malone Road area. I felt a surge of excitement and a little, but not much, apprehension. They all had anglicised names, Rachel and Florence, for example, but African names were also listed as secondary names. Three of them were older than me and two – a boy and a girl – younger.

I called Chris to tell him the news and then I sent a text to my brothers as I wanted to keep them informed each step of the way. Damien and Ciaran were delighted whereas Paddy was a little more concerned about where this was all leading. The next step was to type Michael's children's names into a directory enquiry website that held addresses and electoral rolls in Northern Ireland and across Britain. I typed in the names in turn and ended up with a list of nine addresses in the greater London area. I started to shake.

I contacted Tony at Radio 4 and then went to see Maggie, the social worker. I was concerned about the morality of the whole exercise. I didn't want to wreck anyone's life and I didn't want it to turn out like an episode of *EastEnders* with me showing up on someone's doorstep in the dead of night. Maggie remained calm and detached. She had seen this all before. I told her that I was going to write a letter and send it to the nine addresses because I could tell that the children had lived at these addresses as recently as 2003. Some of the names were listed at more than one of the addresses suggesting that some of them had moved around. Maggie gave me invaluable advice: 'Before you contact these people you need to be very careful and you need to follow some rules. Rule one is that you cannot tell these people who you are or what your relationship is with them.'

'Why not?' I asked.

'Because you don't have the right to just blurt out that you are their brother.'

This made perfect sense. Her second piece of advice presented me with more of a practical challenge. 'Do not tell them any lies,' she said. 'If you lie at the start, you will have real problems trying to build up a relationship with them if that is your intention. Is that your intention? Do you really want to get to know them?'

'Yes.'

The problem was that while I had these addresses I still had no idea where my father was or even if he was still alive. How could I ask them about my father without setting off alarm bells in their heads as to who I was? And if they asked me how could I answer without lying? I had planned to say that I was researching a programme for the BBC. Beyond that, I hadn't thought it through too much.

I composed a diplomatic, friendly letter that said little about me or my motives but that did ask for information about Michael Ekue, whom I knew to be a medical student and who used to live in Belfast. I made nine copies and then sent it out to the nine addresses I had found on the internet. I added my mobile number and email address at the bottom of the letter.

Little over a day later on a dark and wet Friday night, I checked my emails and discovered one that read: 'The man you were asking about is my father, Doctor Ekue. Why do you want to contact him? Adenike (friends call me Nike).' My emotions, never far from the surface at this point in my life, almost overwhelmed me. I was elated. I wanted to rush out into the street to tell the world, my neighbours or just anyone who happened to be passing my window. Not only did I now have contact from a brand-new younger sister but she seemed courteous – referring to Doctor Ekue, she didn't use his first name – and friendly, giving her full name but adding a chatty 'friends call me Nike' in parenthesis.

I was thrilled and immediately informed my brothers and Chris before contacting Tony. I was alive with excitement and wanted to phone this thrilling new presence in my life straight-away, but a realisation deflated my euphoria: Nike didn't give her number, so I couldn't speak to her. Almost instantly I realised that such a call would be a fanciful notion, anyway. What would we say after 'Hello'? I would ask how she was doing and she might do the same but after that she might ask who I was and why I was interested in contacting her father.

I needed to speak to Maggie. On the following Monday,

when she was back at work, I contacted her. 'Why can't I tell any lies?' I asked again.

'Because you'll undermine any basis of trust going forward. They may decide that you are untrustworthy and a liar and cease all contact. You can't afford to give them any reason to back off.'

'Well, then, why can't I tell them the truth?'

'Because you don't know what they have been told. They may have been living a lie for forty years. Perhaps your father has managed to keep his indiscretions secret from his family,' Maggie explained. 'They may not know of your existence and you have no right to walk into their lives all guns blazing. Or, it may be that they suspect something and that his wife, if she is still alive, suspects something. If you're married to someone for over forty years, you're going to have a good idea if they have been having affairs or not, especially when you're married to someone as reckless as your father seems to have been,' she added.

And so, with Maggie's advice, I adopted a very measured approach. I emailed a response to Nike that gave little away about me except that I was a journalist and that it would be great if my contact details could be sent to her father. I also asked if I could have his. 'Please be positive, please be positive,' I prayed. But this email was met with a cooler response, Nike's reply simply stated: 'I will tell my father.' The sense of excitement had gone and the tone was more business-like. In her emails she had referred to him as 'Doctor Ekue' and 'my father'. Why did she refer to him as Doctor Ekue? She seemed respectful, proud, courteous, devoted even. She never used the word 'dad'. She did not give me any contact details for her father and she did not sign off in a friendly manner. I was disappointed.

I waited to hear from her again. Having received an almost instant response from her initially I got frustrated when I turned on my computer several times each day, checked my emails and saw that nothing had come through. I was shocked that a situation I thought I had under control could get me so angry.

Who needs a father anyway? I was a forty-year-old man now – what was in it for me? What does it mean to have a father? A role model? I had had my mum for that. She had put food on the table, she had dispensed wise advice about how the world would be and how I could defend myself, present myself and treat others. She had provided an education for me as best she could and, when I got myself into a corner, she had supported me in a way that few others did. This is as it should be. She was my mum and that's what a mother does, I suppose. But what did a father do? Well, in my experience he had done nothing, other than have an affair with my mum. My father hadn't been there for any of the big moments in my life, so why should I want to meet him now?

Up until my late thirties I held the view that my identity was fixed and unshakeable. I was an Irish republican from the Falls Road. A black Irish republican. I had told Mum that this was the bottom line and that everything else was of little importance. Now, I knew that this was no longer true for me. I was becoming increasingly aware that, except for family and good friends, people had always assumed that I didn't really belong, despite my strong sense of identity. When I was a child I would pray that British Army foot patrols would be all white. If they were all white, I reasoned, they may well abuse me with racist comments but at least the racism would be from them and I would be the victim in the eyes of people of Beechmount. I could handle that. What I found harder to handle was hearing Irish people abusing black soldiers because, although I felt the same way about the British Army as they did, I felt let down by their insults because I was black. Even as an adult, I had often thought twice about watching football matches in bars in the Falls Road area because the other men watching would make racist comments about black players in the heat of the game. In Castlereagh detectives had asked whether I had let the IRA leave the weapons at my house in an attempt to 'fit in' and even some fellow republicans had said that the struggle wasn't really my fight. I wrestled with the sense that I was not always considered, unconditionally, as part of the Irish republican community in which I was raised and which meant so much to me. Finding my father was part of a quest to find out who I really was and where I really came from.

Autumn slipped towards Christmas without any further contact and Maggie and I had a few discussions. It seemed clear that while it wasn't my place to reveal the truth to Nike, I might have to, as gently as possible, let her in on the secret.

We resolved that I would write a letter to my father and, because I had no address or contact details for him, I would send it to my new sister in London but ask her not to open it. She was to forward it on to my father unread. Of course, I had no guarantee that she would not open it and I could not be sure that it would ever find its way to my father.

I foolishly sat down to write a letter that I imagined would take an hour or so. A week later I was still trying to find the right words and the right tone. Sometimes I became angry because of what Mum had gone through or because I had been neglected – in the broadest sense of the word – by my father. The letter sounded hostile and the tone was too judgemental. I knew that if I allowed my anger to show, his daughter, clearly proud of him, might want to protect him. She might refuse to believe the story and throw the letter away, resolving never to mention it to him. I needed Maggie's wisdom and when I called her she gave me one of the best bits of advice I had ever received: 'You have to write a letter to your father explaining what you know and that you would like to meet him. Tell him this can be done discreetly and that you have no desire to hurt or upset his family. However, you have to be realistic, Nike might open the letter. What you need to do is write the letter so well that if she does read it, by the time she gets to the end of the last sentence, she really likes you.'

In an instant Maggie had outlined the style and tone of literally, the letter of my life. I planned to enclose photocopies of my birth certificate, the ledger entry for St Joseph's Baby Home, the letters my father had written to Mum as well as my letter. I waited until early January and then sent the package off with an extra detail at the end – I informed my father that I did not want things to drag out unnecessarily, therefore I was imposing a deadline of 31 January 2007. If I didn't hear anything back from him I would try a different approach to resolve the matter. This was a hint to my father that I would be taking control of the situation and that he could not spin the whole process out. I sent off the package. I immediately worried about the reactions. Would I cause a family crisis? Might I shock people who had no idea of their father's double life? Would they go into denial? I would get my answer in three weeks.

On Tuesday 30 January 2007 I went to buy a 'Get well soon' card in a city-centre shop for my uncle Al who was seriously ill in hospital. While I was there my phone rang. 'Who are you?' came the shout down the phone. Although I did not know who *exactly* was speaking, I knew instinctively what this was about and why he was angry. It was one of my half brothers calling from London. 'Who do you think you are?' he shouted. 'Are you trying to wreck our family?' I was trying to pay for the card at the till. It was half past six in the evening. This caller was hostile and my fears about the pain and tension my package might cause seemed to have been well founded. I tried to pacify him: 'Calm down, calm down. There's nothing to worry about ... Can you ... Would you let me speak ...? Look, please calm down a second.'

The caller's accent – part greater London, part African – confirmed to me that he was my brother, but he seemed to have no idea who I was, which confused me. Surely he had read the letter and seen the supporting evidence? I glanced at my watch to confirm the date, 30 January. Surely he knew the deadline was the following day? If he knew that he must also know who I was. Just my luck, I thought. They had opened the package intended for my father and didn't like what I had sent them.

Relentless questions were aimed into my ear, rapid fire. 'Who are you? What do you want with us? Who do you think you are?'

'If you let me speak I can explain things and there is nothing to worry about. Can you calm down and stop shouting, please?' I asked quietly.

Eventually he calmed down but interrupted me almost every time I spoke. Having calmed him, I panicked about the momentous news I had for him. I felt that I needed to speak to Maggie. I was worried that if I said the wrong thing he would hang up and contact would be lost. His number had not flashed up on my screen when the phone rang.

'Look, can I ask what your name is?'

'No!'

'Why not?'

'You don't get to ask who I am. You tell me what *you* want and who *you* are. Why do you want to know about my family?'

I hesitated. I didn't want to lie but I wasn't ready to blurt out truths that, once told, could not be retracted or forgotten.

'Are you a doctor?' he asked.

'No.'

'Are you a journalist?'

'Yes.' I needed to buy time but worried that he would sever this lifeline to my father. 'You must know who I am. You rang me and you got the package I sent a few weeks ago?'

'That package is on its way back to you by now, unopened!'

'Why didn't you open it? If you'd opened it, all of the questions you've asked me would be answered.'

'Are you serious? We're not going to open a package from bloody Belfast! There could be anything in that!'

I found it hard to believe that they hadn't opened the package and seen the birth certificate, the letters from our father to my mum, the photocopies from the baby home. I had worked on the assumption that they had opened them and were going to deny everything. 'Can you do me a favour? Will you let me call you tomorrow? Can I have your number?'

'No! What sort of man are you? Who do you need to speak to? Who? What the ... ?'

'There's someone I need to speak to first,' I said.

'If you don't tell me what is going on right now and who you are I'll hang up and you will never get anywhere near our father.'

'My uncle is very ill,' I said. 'I'm outside the hospital about to go and see him. Can you please calm down, let me do this and if you call tomorrow lunchtime I promise I will answer all your questions.' I wasn't at the hospital or anywhere near it but as luck had it, not one but two ambulances, sirens wailing, flew by me at speed along Belfast's main shopping street. He could hear them in the background.

'Oh, why didn't you say?' he said, his voice calming down. 'Of course. Go do what you have to do.'

At last! He sounded human and reasonable. We agreed to speak at noon the following day. This would give me time to speak to Maggie on Wednesday morning.

I told Maggie the details including my belief that I had gone as far as I could with the 'no-lies' policy. I also told her about the family's stipulation that I would never get to my father without telling them on the phone who I was. My link to my father was fragile. The next phone call was going to make or break my search but equally it could break the trust between members of a family. It could break up a marriage. I didn't want to hurt anyone but I felt that the time had come to tell the truth. 'They have forced you into a corner,' said Maggie, 'and the only thing you can do is explain that the information you have is for your father and that if he knew that his children were demanding to hear it, he may not approve. Tell them that and if they insist on hearing your story regardless, then you have done all you can and you can tell them.' This seemed like sensible advice.

At precisely noon the next day my home telephone rang. It was Kaizi – my brother who had called the day before. I explained my concerns to him but he was still keen to hear the story. I drew a deep breath: 'In 1965, my mum, Peggy Brannigan, met a man called Michael, a doctor from Ghana at a dance in central Belfast. They became friendly and had an affair. As a result of that affair Peggy became pregnant. She had a baby called Tim. I believe you are one of Michael's sons which would mean that, right now, you are talking to your brother...' Following a brief silence there was a briefer response: 'Wow! Right...' I explained to him why I had been so cautious about telling him my story. As he spoke the postman arrived and through my living room window I could see the package I had sent to London had been sent back. It had not been opened.

'Have you got paperwork to prove all of this?' he asked.

I told him that the truth lay in the package that they hadn't opened. His next comment was unexpected. 'What I'm going to do is go away and think about this,' he said in a considered way. 'I won't tell anyone as I just want to allow it to sink in, to consider it and then think about how we move this forward. There's just one problem. My mum doesn't know any of this and she mustn't know. She isn't well and this could be the thing that sends her over the edge.'

We agreed to hang up and speak again the next day. However, only two hours later I received a second, even more surprising call from Foli, another brother. 'Hi Tim, this is Foli. I am Kaizi's older brother. He told me what you said. Isn't this what life's all about? Life is about the unexpected, the big issues. This is something that, if we handle it properly and sensitively, can be a very positive experience. We can all learn a lot from this.' He spoke in this unerringly positive way for quite a while and I almost giggled with happiness. 'Our father is a great man, Tim. Really impressive. You'll really like him when you meet him. He's the most intelligent man I've ever met.'

'That's just it, Foli. I want to meet him.'

'You will. If we work together and move this forward it can be a life-changing experience. However, we have to be sensitive. Our mum isn't well. She's very ill and this? Well, one step at a time ...'

He asked me a few questions about myself. I was circumspect with my answers but didn't tell any lies. I simply said that I had been around the block a few times and that I was a journalist. He told me that he and Kaizi had recently moved to India with their families. They owned a computer company that exported software back to Europe. It sounded quite impressive. There were three sisters but one of them, he informed me, was a bit headstrong and that I would have to take him on trust that they wouldn't be telling her about all of this just yet.

Foli informed me that when they were children in Belfast he had a sense that his father might have been having an affair as they had left Belfast unexpectedly and suddenly. They had been getting prepared for school there and before they knew it they were in London and there was some tension within the family. 'I think we had an idea about an affair but we didn't know of any child,' he said. 'Does my father know you exist?'

'Can I just clarify something?' I said. 'Before you ask me any questions about *our* father, you need to be sure that you are ready to hear the answers, OK?' I cautioned.

'OK,' Foli said.

'Yes, he knows I exist,' I said. 'He saw me at least once when I was a toddler and he and Mum discussed my welfare, future and education.' I stopped myself from saying too much too soon. I was aware that the situation could still blow up in my face or that signs of anger on my part could put an end to all contact.

'What do you want out of all this, Tim?' Foli asked.

'I'm not sure. I don't expect to be round for Christmas dinner. But I want to meet my father,' I said. 'We've had very different experiences,' I continued. 'He wasn't there for birthdays, Christmases or the first day at school and those are things that can't easily be made up. My relationship with our father – I can't get used to speaking about having a father, I don't know what to call him – will never be the same as yours.

I know that. I guess it would be good if we could be like cousins. The odd call, the odd birthday card and a visit now and again. I don't know ...

'That sounds good, Tim.'

We agreed to keep in regular contact. He explained that the issues raised were sensitive and that they weren't things to be discussed with our father on the telephone. He would rather raise them face-to-face. I agreed.

As the weeks slipped by contact was patchy and Foli agreed to allow Ama, the eldest daughter, to take over maintaining contact given that she and I were, geographically at least, closer to each other and Foli was busy trying to get his company up and running in a foreign country. Some weeks after I had spoken to the brothers Ama rang me. We had a long chat that was friendly and even warm. It was certainly emotional. She asked quite early on if our father knew of my existence. I said yes and as I explained about being placed in the baby home she gasped but made no comment.

She had some surprises of her own. She said that when she received my letter the previous autumn she knew instantly what it all meant. She'd said nothing to her siblings about her suspicions. Ama indicated that there had been previous indiscretions and that her mother was aware of them: 'Years ago we lived in Zambia and we knew a nurse who worked there. She died of Aids. After her death, my father gave the family a sum of money to help with the children. I was talking with my mother and from nowhere she said, "I think your father had an affair with that nurse".'

She confirmed what Foli had said, that they had been due to attend a prep school in Belfast but without warning they were whisked away to boarding schools in England. They were educated in the south west of England as their father considered London to be too rough. They later moved to various African countries as our father pursued his medical work. I told her that the one thing my mum had asked of our father was that he provide for my education; that she had never asked him for money for herself, only that Michael provide for the child he had with her in the manner he provided for his other children.

I couldn't help but wonder what would have happened if I had been taken out of a working-class boys' secondary school to be educated privately in a boarding school in a quiet, rural location. Things might have turned out differently if I'd been at a school where the teachers didn't make racist 'jokes' or suggest that I had lied simply because I happened to compose a poem that rhymed. And of course, in my school, the IRA occasionally made an appearance, ordering us out at times of political crisis. It could all have been so different, I suppose, but whether it would have been better for me is another question.

I was delighted and a little apprehensive when Ama agreed without hesitation to meet me when I was next in London. She wanted to keep our rendezvous relatively quiet and said that she would not be telling the middle, hot-headed sister, Adzoa. We agreed to keep in touch with a view to meeting as soon as possible.

Despite Ama's best efforts to urge my father to make contact with me, days slipped into weeks and there was still no call from him. Occasionally she'd ring, email or text to say that he would be calling. But the call never came. I got angry but had to bite my lip, as it was hardly her fault. Bit by bit though she revealed significant details about the nature of her relationship with our father. Once, thinking aloud, she said: 'This is Tuesday ... goes to meeting Thursday night. Sunday. Yes, Sunday! He'll be going to church. I'll try to get him as he drives to church.' I expressed some frustration. 'Can't you just call him up, Ama?'

'I don't want to ring him if I think he's with Mum. I need to wait until he's not near her.'

'When you call him, will you tell him I'm angry that he has been promising to call but not been doing it?'

'I don't think I could use the word "angry" with father.'

I got the sense that he was remote from his children and that he was a disciplinarian. My blood boiled. What sort of man was this? Who did he think he was?

Ama rang again to say he would call but I didn't hold out too much hope. I waited at home and this time, close to the appointed time, my phone rang.

'Hello?'

'Hello. Is that Tim?'

'Yes.'

'This is Dr Ekue.'

'Hello. Thanks for calling. How are you?' I said, struggling to contain my excitement.

'I'm fine ...'

He spoke deliberately with a deep voice. There were awkward silences and I struggled to know what to say. What could I say to a man about whom I knew so little and for whom I had such strong, often conflicting, feelings? What would Mum want me to do? Should I mention her at all? I didn't need to.

'And how is Peggy Brannigan?' I wondered why he used her full name.

'I'm sorry to tell you this but Mum passed away a few years ago. She had a brain tumour.'

'I am very sorry to hear that. I'd like to offer you my condolences. She was a lovely woman. A very decent woman.'

He sounded sincere. I was moved by his sympathetic remarks. This gesture wrong-footed me as part of me wanted to be firm with him. I told him I expected to meet him and that it was important that he told the other children that everything I had been telling them was true. He told me not to worry about the children, that he would speak to them.

As we spoke on my landline, my mobile phone beeped and I could see I had a text message. I read it. It was from Ama: 'I spoke to my father about you. Welcome to the family, brother.' I was overwhelmed and struggled to focus on my very first conversation with my father. He asked where I lived and when I told him my address he recognised it – it was only yards from where he used to meet Mum at the long-gone Broadway cinema. The rest of the call was small talk about my career and circumstances. He was driving and began to hint that he would have to call me back as he wasn't able to speak properly.

'I'll just call you Michael,' I said, not wanting to ask his permission. Calling him 'dad' was not an option – it was far too familiar, friendly and more than anything, false. He was not 'dad'. I also considered 'father' too awkward; too deferential. I didn't get the sense that he wanted to hear any phrase that suggested bloodlines or family ties. I don't think he wanted any language, gestures or behaviour that he could not walk away from in a heartbeat. This, after all, was a man who was able to walk away from his own child, leaving me in a home while he went back to family; his medical career; his busy social diary. He hesitated for long enough to rile me. Cheerily, I repeated, 'I'm just calling you Michael.' And with that the conversation drew to a close.

I immediately contacted Ama and chatted to her in a breathless fashion. She told me that he had phoned her just before he called me and that they had talked about me. Major hurdles had been overcome. I was going over to London to meet Tony at Radio 4, so I could meet Ama when I was there. My life, I felt, was about to take off again.

On a cool, wet day in London in the spring of 2007, I met my older sister, Ama. She was a large woman, dressed in ordinary clothes. She had a lovely smile. As I approached her I did a quick scan for resemblances but saw none. Then I remembered that I looked very much like some of my brothers in Belfast so it was unlikely that I'd look like Ama or the others. I had been sent a few pictures of Foli and Kaizi via email. We hugged and exchanged a kiss on the cheek before heading for coffee on Oxford Street. I was dressed casually but was, I felt, presentable. I wanted to make a good impression. She seemed reserved and not given to overwhelming affection. I, too, kept my emotions in check. We discussed many issues but I did not reveal my republican background because I didn't want to alarm her or give her any reason to walk away from the whole situation. She told me about a serious medical condition that affected some, but not all, of the family. I had to go and get blood tests for sickle cell anaemia, a condition that affects many Africans and Afro-Caribbeans. The condition makes the blood thicken to the point where it can coagulate in the veins leading to life-threatening clots. Those severely affected by it cannot exert themselves too much or carry out strenuous exercise. My doctors told me that I was fine and it would only affect my children if I married an African woman or a girl of African origin.

Ama and I spoke about ordinary matters even though the meeting itself was extraordinary. Ama had fond memories of Belfast and a friend she knew. She even remembered the friend's address in the Malone area of south Belfast. I asked about Adzoa, the strong-minded sister. They spoke about her as though she had a ferocious temper but I suspected that she could not be as bad as they said. They worried that she would react badly to the news of my existence and would create problems. I asked if the other sisters knew that she was meeting me. She said that she may have mentioned the possibility of a meeting some months back but that they did not know that anything was happening that day. This annoyed me. Too many secrets, I thought.

Then she casually mentioned our father's trips to Scotland. 'He goes to Scotland every year.'

'Why?'

'He goes to his lodge meetings.'

'What lodge?' I said. 'My story's mad enough without finding out I've an Orangeman for a da!' She smiled slightly nervously and explained that he was actually a Freemason.

I walked Ama to the bus for her journey home. We said our goodbyes and I was delighted when, some weeks later, Ama's daughters rang me to wish me a happy birthday. They even called me 'Uncle Tim' during the phone call. They sent a birthday card and a family portrait too. I thought this was a magnificent gesture. We agreed to keep working on establishing contact between our father and myself. She was friendly, if reserved, and seemed to be quite positive about my goals.

Throughout the spring of 2007 I persevered in trying to get my father to contact me on some sort of regular basis. I wasn't looking for daily contact, simply a commitment to acknowledge my existence, to treat me with respect and to take an interest in me. I had his mobile number but had agreed not to call him too often in case his wife picked up the phone. Instead, I would send him texts that he could respond to in his own time. I began to get frustrated and hurt at his silences and what I felt was indifference. 'You should be delighted that I am showing the discretion and patience I am with you,' I said during one of our rare phone calls. 'After what you have done, I might be justified in rampaging through your life without regard to your feelings and the feelings of anyone close to you. Many other fathers have found themselves with very angry resentful children on their hands, understandably so. I'm being reasonable but you aren't meeting me halfway.' He said nothing. I told him that I was planning to come to Africa and again he showed little in the way of reaction. I guessed he was not overjoyed by the prospect.

Tony at Radio 4 indicated that the timing was up to me. I spoke to Ama on the phone and told her that I wanted to meet our father. 'Well, I know he's busy at the minute and I don't think he has any plans to be in England until the end of the year, November maybe?'

'You don't understand, I intend to go to him in Africa. The waiting is over. I'm going.' This news was greeted with total silence. I didn't care. My father responded to my plans by doing what he did best, going to ground and hoping that I would just leave him alone. I spoke to Foli and told him that I planned to go to Africa to meet our father. 'I need you to get him to phone me,' I said. Foli told me that our father had asked, 'What does he want?' I interpreted this as meaning 'Why won't he go away?'

I sent my father more texts outlining my plans and, in as friendly a tone as I could muster, telling him that I didn't intend to cause trouble and that he should meet me at my hotel. He sent texts back, occasionally, promising calls that never came. By the end of May I resolved to book a flight and Tony agreed to accompany me. As a journalist I appreciated the importance of getting my father on the record; the emotional climax of the tale; father and son reunited. But what would my father make of a man from the BBC being there? Was this the right move? Could I put the demands of the programme ahead of the emotionally charged impact of finally meeting my father? Should I worry about the BBC's expectations?

I decided that the most important issue was my desire to do the right thing by my new family. I wanted the relationship to build and grow and not end with my meeting my father being reduced to the 'money shot' of a documentary. Tony and I agreed that the first meeting had to be private and that after that I would raise the issue of the documentary and see if he would be willing to participate, giving his side of the story.

The flights were booked for the 4 July 2007. I joked to a friend that it would be renamed 'Dependants Day' for the purposes of this trip. Ama and Foli became harder to contact as they realised I was serious about going to Africa. My sense of determination was mixed with an element of self-righteousness: 'I'm doing this for my mum,' I thought. 'She wanted to know what happened to you and she wanted you to see that she brought me up the best way she could under extraordinary circumstances.' One minute I wanted to be an easygoing guy who had a philosophical attitude to life and in a heartbeat I became angry again. In the weeks leading up to the trip, I wrestled with these emotions. I worried too that my father didn't ring in the run-up to my departure and I hid from Tony the fact that we were planning to fly to a different continent even though I had no idea where my father lived.

Eventually, I told Tony as he would have to answer to his bosses for a hefty expenses bill if we came back with nothing.

He said that he knew there was a risk of getting nothing but it was a risk worth taking. I felt relieved. I decided that if my father didn't contact me on day one we would leave no stone unturned to find him.

My father was a well-known doctor who had given years of service to the United Nations seeking a cure for malaria. There would be people at the main hospitals that would know him, surely? And as he was a member of the Freemasons and the Rotary Club we could visit their headquarters and make en-quiries there too. The BBC name would also open a few doors, I thought.

And so we made our way to Heathrow airport. In the hours before the flight, I checked my emails to see if Ama or Foli had sent any replies to me about the trip and whether they had received any instruction from our father about a time or a location for a meeting. There were no replies. I got angry and sent an email telling them that I was about to fly out. I suggested that their stance conflicted with all of the 'Welcome to the family' texts and 'Isn't this what life's all about?' phone calls. I could hardly contain my emotions although I calmed down a bit as we got on the plane. I surveyed the scene. There were mostly black people on the plane. That was a first for me. Many of them seemed to be tourists bringing back trophies of a trip to the west, wearing designer-label clothes with pride and no little ostentation.

I sent a series of texts to my father during the journey. 'I'm flying to London.' 'I'm at Heathrow.' 'I am staying at a hotel in Accra.' 'I arrive tonight around 10 p.m.' One of the last read, 'There is no need to feel anxious. Meet me at my hotel – only you need know of our meeting.'

We stayed at a business-standard hotel in Accra, Ghana's capital city. I had been in the developing world, or 'Third World' as it used to be called, when I visited Honduras and Nicaragua seven years before but I was still unsure of what to expect. I worried over the small domestic matters. Would it be hot? Yes. Were there proper pavements and roads? Yes – and they even had four-lane roads with traffic lights and road markings. I suspected the lights and road markings were there as public art because no one seemed pay them any attention. Driving in Ghana seemed to be an exercise in rigging up your battered car with a car radio or sound system that must be played at full volume. The only other essential item that any car needs in Ghana is a functioning horn – not because it alerts pedestrians to speeding cars as they attempt to cross the road, but because it acts as an indicator. Cars speed towards junctions, slow down – well slow down a little – and then, in the manner of dodgem cars at a fairground, the drivers point their car roughly in the direction they want to go and then drive towards it beeping the car horn all the way.

'Why don't you use the indicators?' I asked one taxi driver.

'Cos, I got this,' he said as he honked his car horn.

On the occasions when the traffic did slow down, faces young and old, male and female, appeared at the car windows with a speed that seemed at odds with the tiredness etched on every face. And why wouldn't they be tired? They would get up at 4 or 5 a.m. and take overcrowded buses from the edge of town or the countryside and travel to Accra in the forlorn hope of finding buyers for a range of goods I hadn't seen since looking in the cupboard under the sink in the 1970s. 'You mean you don't need a packet of Omo soap powder?' they seemed to say when we shook our heads. 'Then, how about these dish mops, tea towels, Brillo pads, scouring pads, tin openers? Or what about this towel with the Manchester United logo on it? These cups? Take a mug, it's official Liverpool FC merchandise.' They were persistent too, following our taxi along busy roads until a gap allowed us to speed away. Then they turned to the next car.

Tony and I hung around the hotel waiting on a call that was never going to come. I sent my father several friendly texts but one had a deliberately ambiguous ending: 'I'm closer than you think'. I wanted to force his hand and this phrase suggested that I knew where he lived. Or at least that's what I wanted it to suggest. This, I knew would be the worst-case scenario for him. That evening Tony and I decided to go to our rooms to relax. Around 5 p.m. the phone in my room rang. 'Mr Brannigan, there's a man at reception to see you.'

Under African Skies

After years of unanswered questions, it came down to this. My father, a man I'd never met but whom my mum admired, and possibly loved, was finally ready to meet me. I wondered how long it would take me to recognise him. Would there be a resemblance? Would we hit it off immediately? Should I hug him? Despite all these unanswered questions, I didn't feel nervous or anxious and I was delighted that I didn't feel angry. I was just happy and relieved – I bounded down the stairs.

There he was. He was wearing one of those long cotton African tops with no collar. He was big-shouldered, solid-looking and despite sitting down he seemed tall. He was much blacker than me. He had a strong, proud face and his hair was styled in a crew cut. He looked composed, powerful, and, in spite of his greying hairline, much younger than his seventy or so years.

'My God! What height are you?' I asked.

His blackness was lightened by a smile.

'I think you are taller than me,' he said slowly and deeply.

'Hello Michael, it's great to meet you,' I said leaning forward, gauging the strength of his handshake. He stood up. He was wearing charcoal grey trousers with a sharp crease. They were the perfect length; no socks were exposed but they weren't gathered on his shiny black shoes either. This man was concerned about appearances.

'Sit down, Michael. Look, I'm just going to call you Michael, OK?' I swept an open palm across the six feet of space between us. There was no debate about how I should address him. His hands were on his thighs. He rolled them open to show me his palms then placed them back on his thighs. I took this to mean, 'Whatever suits you'.

'I'm here because of my mum, Peggy. Peggy Brannigan. All of my life she wanted me to meet you. I could take or leave the idea for most of my life, to be honest with you, but things change, I guess. Situations change and last year the opportunity to come out here arose, so here I am. I'm as surprised as you. Beyond that I have no real agenda ...' I tried to sound light and cheery. I thought of Tony in his room. I hoped he would come down, but not too soon.

'So, how are you, Michael?' I said.

'I'm fine. I ... I am sorry I'm late. I had to drive down the coast. I had to make sure the men are doing what they are supposed to. I'm having some property built ...'

'Property,' he said. Not a house but 'property'? Was it a holiday home? A hotel? Property was a vague word, deliberately so, I suspected. I added this to the information that came from Foli in a call a few months previously, that he was hoping to entice our father to 'invest in a business venture, nothing to do with our own company, just a little sideline'. This man was doing well for himself, by African standards – by any standards, I think.

'And how is your wife?'

'She is fine. People are ... looking after her ...' He said. He seemed to choose his words carefully. Nurses, I suspected. He spoke in the plural; 'people' were looking after her.

'Getting here has been quite a journey, Michael. Growing up in Belfast is quite difficult for a black kid. It wasn't easy but I've done OK, I think. I hope.' I laughed nervously.

'And you stayed in Beechmount?'

'Yeah, I live near the Royal, Beechmount Avenue.'

'I know it. I used to drive around the Falls and the Shankill when I was a young doctor. Even during the Troubles. Through the barricades! Ha ha ha!' I didn't expect such a belly laugh. He laughed with an African accent. This made me laugh. '"Yes Doctor Ekue, you can come through," they would say at the barricades. "It's Mrs Smith, she's not well, doctor. You can come through, no problem."'

'We got involved in the Troubles, you know, Michael. Mum was a republican. We're a republican family.'

'I know. Peggy was very strong. Definitely not British! Ha ha ha!' He slapped his thigh at the memory of discussions long gone, but seemingly not forgotten. 'She was definitely not British!'

'I've had the odd run-in with the Brits myself. I'll tell you now so you don't find out in any shocking way, but I was in jail...' A slow nod of the head invited me to continue. 'I was caught with rifles and grenades at our house.'

'In Beechmount?'

'Yes, Mica Drive. It was 1990. I'd just come home from studying in England. I had just graduated and come home for some proper food and the next thing you know I'm in Crumlin Road Prison.'

'How...? How did you...? Who...?'

'The IRA called to the door. I was home alone...'

I took him back to 1990 and through to 1995 over the next few minutes, emphasising the unique nature of life as a political prisoner and the fact that the armed struggle was about identity and self-determination. I didn't want him to think his son had done anything he should be ashamed of. I wondered how on earth I'd got onto the subject. It was partly nerves and partly having nothing prepared. Still, I could see that my stories of jail had a captive audience. 'But I'm not bitter about it,' I said. 'I don't hate the men who called. I certainly don't hate the IRA and since then I've become a journalist so, you know, swings and roundabouts...'

'Ha ha. Yes...'

I relaxed and remembered that there was a bar tucked away

behind a door in the corner, 'Would you like a drink, Michael?' He hesitated but eventually agreed to take one, mindful that he had to drive home. Early on I said that I'd like to see as much of him as I could during my few days here. 'We can meet anywhere you want, discreetly.' I told him. 'Here or in a bar somewhere.'

We talked some more and Michael opened up a little. I think he began to trust that I was not trying to make his life difficult. 'I'll tell you what my greatest achievement was. It was putting all of my children through private education,' he said before pausing. 'It's a good achievement,' I said but I was struggling to contain my true feelings. I just looked at him and nodded. 'In fact, that is where most of my money went to. I spent it all on education for my children.' He seemed to be inviting me to shower him with praise when actually I was feeling quite uncomfortable. Had he forgotten Mum's only request of him, that he help with my education? I thought it better to change the subject rather than get into anything contentious when we'd only just met.

'There is one thing I should tell you' I said. 'I didn't travel here alone. I'm making a documentary for BBC Radio about my life. There's a producer here. He's up in his room and we would like you to take part in the show – if you want to, that is. He could record some of our conversation, although it need not be anything especially personal.' I wondered how he would take this news. He paused for a moment. 'I could never appear on the BBC on any recording. I'm a registered doctor in three countries. We have ethics. Codes of conduct. I could never talk about ... all of this.' Ethics? Codes of conduct? Who was he kidding? I thought. I decided to keep these thoughts to myself for now. 'I'm not here to put pressure on you. I'm just happy to meet you, Michael. It has to be your decision, although Tony will be disappointed and, speaking as a journalist, it would be fantastic to get your side of the story.' He said nothing but the fact that he had matched all the fingertips of his right hand against the corresponding fingers of his left and raised his forefingers to his lips suggested that he was either praying for guidance or unconsciously keeping his lips sealed.

'So, you're a Freemason? Are you the token black guy?' I said, laughing. 'What on earth are you doing?'

'It's not like you think,' he said.

'I think it's very conservative,' I butted in to make sure he was in no doubt about my views. 'I'm not worried about funny handshakes, the conservatism is enough for me.'

'It's a social thing. The books are all wrong ... all those rumours...' he said.

And so, in an empty hotel bar we talked about anything and everything, from his views on global politics to why I hadn't married. Eventually he had to go home. Night came down in the blink of an eye. We emerged from the lobby into a balmy breeze that felt like warm water. Should I hug him? I wondered. I didn't feel I could. We agreed to meet the next day. He shook my hand and walked to a battered old car that stood out among the more prestigious vehicles in the car park. I wasn't convinced this was the sum total of his car collection. 'It was great to meet you, don't let me down tomorrow.'

My father came back the following evening as arranged. We sat by the swimming pool and the starry African skies provided a suitably magical backdrop to a joyously relaxed meeting. I invited Tony along so that he could satisfy himself that my father couldn't be persuaded to take part in the programme. The three of us had a wide-ranging chat about politics, George Bush, the War on Terror, the Middle East and Africa's problems, Ireland and Britain. What we did not discuss was my father's relationship with Mum, his attitude to my birth, his broken pledges about my education or indeed any matters pertaining directly to me. We did not discuss his actions after I was born or the many years during which he had played no part in my life. I wanted to know what he had to say about these issues but I decided that I should build up a relationship with him first. We agreed that we would meet again before I flew back, probably on Sunday afternoon.

On Saturday, Tony recorded my thoughts as we visited the old slave fort that eventually became the prison in Accra. It was a horrifying place. Occasionally, I would send my father a text letting him know where we were and when we would be back at the hotel. Heading back through the market we discovered an Irish bar of sorts. It claimed to be an Irish bar but was little more than a first-floor, gloomily-lit room with a balcony overlooking a particularly busy part of town where rowdy children and rowdier adults egged each other on in mock fights and whistled at women. We sat on the balcony and were served by a surly waitress who tutted each time she was called upon, probably because she had to squeeze between crates of Guinness to reach the bar. On reflection, this seemed to be an authentic Irish bar experience, after all.

We rounded the day off at two hotel bars where the wealthy Ghanaian elite mixed with Europeans and Americans. At our own hotel, I chatted to the barman. Three members of staff had asked if either of us could get them into Britain or Ireland. The security guard at our hotel made the same request while I stood outside texting friends in Ireland. 'What would you do in Ireland?' I asked.

'This,' he said pointing with his torch at the badge of the security firm sewn to his jacket. 'In Ireland I would make a lot of money. In Ireland this is a good job.'

I could hardly speak. I wanted to help but knew I couldn't.

The reception staff was mainly young women between eighteen and thirty years old. They had beautiful, biblical names. Faith, Charity, Epiphany. 'Our names mean something,' said one. One of the waitresses could have been a model. She glided across the floor and served us with grace and discretion, always making eye contact, always with a big smile. Quietly she broke her silence, 'Can you get me a job where you live?' I took a deep breath and puffed my cheeks trying to think of a good way to give her a negative answer. She sensed that it was a difficulty. 'Oh, it's no big thing. I just mention it in a casual manner,' she said engagingly. As we left

I gave her thirty pounds in English notes when no one else was looking. 'Hide that!' I urged. 'Gone!' she replied.

I asked our barman what his life was like. He had three daughters. He worked horrendously long shifts but was glad of the work. He finished at 3 a.m. and then faced a two-hour bus ride home through the slums and darkness as various members of the hotel staff were dropped off. All of this was for a pittance of a wage. I gave him about four weeks wages from the loose change in my pocket, said good night and went to my room only to discover more Ghanaian change. I brought it down to him along with some sweets, bars of chocolate and crisps that I had bought for myself.

'The money is for you, the sweets are for your girls.' He started to cry and shook my hand, saying something in a local dialect. 'Do you like football?' I asked.

'Yes, very much.'

'Well, if Ireland ever make it to the finals again you must support them, OK?'

'I will, oh yes!'

And with that I left him to clear his empty bar of its last few glasses.

Sunday was a day of restlessness. The heat added to the wearying stress. I sent texts to my father who sent several back promising me that he would try to make it but that he was busy. In the afternoon, I sent him a final text telling him that I had two hours before I had to be at the airport. He replied: 'Stay there as late as you can. I will try to get there.' I was delighted that these seemed to be the words of someone trying to make an effort. We waited until the last minute but then headed to the airport. He never made it.

I regretted that I hadn't asked him the hard questions the moment I'd met him. Easing into the prickly issues slowly seemed to be the best strategy at the time. Meeting him was an unforgettable experience but not getting to ask the big questions made it feel like I was going home empty-handed in some ways. The opportunity to ask these questions would surely come up in future phone calls, though. I felt that the trip had helped to establish a relationship and that I had made a good impression – even if my background was a little unconventional.

My father and I had agreed at our second meeting that we would meet up again in London the next time he came to Britain to see his daughters. There were a couple of phone calls after Ghana but my father soon reverted to type, not answering calls, not returning text messages and being evasive. Since the trip to Africa I had been sending him texts, mostly quite chatty in nature. Sometimes though, after weeks without reply, my frustration would break through: 'You promised you would get in touch. Breaking promises seems to be a habit of yours.' I wrote angry texts and long emails but didn't send them. I didn't have his email address but it was therapeutic nonetheless. He often let the phone ring. I rang him in December, catching him unawares. He spoke of being 'busy' and said he wasn't able to talk. I told him I expected him to meet me in London, even if it was only for a drink or a coffee. I asked him if he thought I was being unreasonable. He didn't give a definitive answer but suggested there were two sides to the story. 'Yes, but for over forty years, you've had the world just where you want it, Michael.' He said he was busy again but promised to call me on Christmas Day.

Until the year before Mum died every Christmas I had ever had was spent at our home. Her Christmas dinner was in itself a Christmas miracle. She spent longer making the gravy and stuffing than other people did making their entire dinner. Since she died, the day had come to haunt me. It was something I faced with a sense of dread. But on Christmas Day 2007, waiting for Michael's call, I felt a sense of excitement about the day again.

As my fibre-optic Christmas tree swirled a kaleidoscope of pleasing lights around my living room, the call came.

'Hello, this is Doctor Ekue.'

'Michael! How are you? Merry Christmas, by the way.'

'And you. Look, I said I would call on Christmas day and so this is me calling. I've called and I hope you have a good day but I have to ...'

'Whoa! Just hold on a minute. Is that it? Are you just clocking in here? Aren't you going to speak to me?'

'About what?' he said. Although this annoyed me at the time, I later thought he probably didn't mean to be provocative.

'About what? Well, about you not meeting me in London when you said you would. I was texting you and I knew you were in London when you didn't reply. I called your phone and it said you were outside the country. You knew I only wanted to meet you in a coffee shop and yet you hadn't the decency to ring or meet me or even acknowledge my texts.'

'I was in London but I was ill and it was all I could do to speak to my children. I was very ill for most of the trip.'

'No! It wasn't "all you could do". You went to Edinburgh, didn't you?'

Silence.

'Didn't you?'

'Yes.'

Then he said something I didn't expect and I didn't know whether to believe him or not. 'I was going to fly to Belfast to see you. I was going to surprise you.'

'When were you planning to do this?' I was incredulous.

'When I was in London. But I was ill so I couldn't do it.'

'You are an extremely selfish, self-serving man, Michael. You can make time for the Freemasons but not for your own son as you promised. What are you in the Freemasons for anyway? They're nothing but a pack of Tories. You're a black man, for God's sake! You claim you were going to fly to Belfast but yet you couldn't even send a text to say "Sorry, I can't make it". It really is all or nothing with you. Sometimes, Michael, you make me very angry. And when I was in Africa you said one of the most shocking things I've ever heard. You told me your greatest achievement was putting your children through private edu-cation. All your children? *All* your children? What about me? I didn't go to a private school. I went to a secondary school on the Falls Road. So don't ever boast to me about your achievements.

Silence.

'Hello?'

'Yes, hello...'

'I am sorry but I am so angry you didn't tell me when you were in London. I could have booked a flight. I have gone to great lengths to make this easy for you but if you think I'm going to say nothing while you ignore me, then you're very much mistaken...

'Are you going to let me speak?' he said

'Please do, Michael. I've waited forty years, flown across the world and you have had very little to say. I have been trying to get a dialogue going. I want you to speak.'

'What would you like me to say?'

'You're an educated man. I shouldn't have to tell you what to say to your son. Shall I ask you a simple question?'

'Yes.'

'OK then. How did you meet my mum?'

'I don't have to answer that.'

'What? Why wouldn't you answer it?'

'That's personal.'

'You are joking? I know it's personal. It's personal to me...'

Making an expansive sweep with my left arm I invited my father thousands of miles away to look across Belfast's panorama. 'I can't imagine there's a family in this whole town in which the children haven't asked that question. "Daddy, how did you meet Mummy?"'

'I don't want to talk about these things. These are things that will just come out in time if we talk normally about other things first. You can't just expect a simple answer to that question,' he said.

'The thing is Michael, I know a lot more than I have told you about your relationship with my mum. She told me in detail all that she knew. So, I know how you met. I'd just like to hear your side of the story.'

'All in good time.'

I was furious with his glib responses, 'And who made you bulletproof?' I asked.

'What do you mean?'

'You're seventy or more. Do you think you you'll be around indefinitely? I'd love to kick back and let all of this happen in a leisurely way but anything could happen to you and then where would I be? And if you do want to talk casually and let things come out over time give me your email address and we can build from there.'

'I don't check emails. Once a week just, maybe.'

'So, I fly to Africa having tracked you down and yet you won't even give me your email address? I'm your son.'

'Let's go slowly.'

'We've had forty years of going slowly.'

'I'm going to have to go now. I told you that I would call you to say hello at Christmas. I have done that.'

'OK. Look I'm sorry but you don't communicate and I get angry. I wasn't like this in Ghana and that's because you came and met me. It was discreet. Perhaps you should reflect on which strategy of yours will be most effective in the long run. After all this time I was expecting something more than "Happy Christmas!" Bye!'

I ended the call and later that evening I sent him a pleasant cheery text. He replied: 'May the Lord bless all of your laudable undertakings.'

That was the last time I heard from my father. I did text him in May 2009 to tell him that I understood that he had been a young man with difficult decisions to make. He has never replied. I'm not certain where he lives, I don't know what he thinks and I don't even know if he's alive. I regret that my brothers and sisters greeted me so warmly, then receded into the shadows. It makes me lose sleep some nights but I always return to a comforting thought – I had a hero for a mother who fought from the day I was born for what she thought was right and what was best for me.

Epilogue

The Radio 4 documentary was broadcast in August 2007 and was very well received by the media. It was repeated on Radio 4 in December of that year and has been broadcast on BBC Radio Ulster several times since. As a result of the documentary, I was approached by several major broadcasters about making documentaries for television in Britain and Ireland and I started working on this book. In February 2008 I called my brother Foli, hoping that he could persuade our father to talk to me so that we could agree about which information should be made public. I also wanted to check some family details, times and dates.

'Hi Foli.'

'Tim. Yes, hi.'

'Are you all well?'

'Yes. What? What is it?'

'Well, look. I just thought it was about time I let you know that I'm working on the book and the thing is, I feel it's only fair to warn you that there's been some media interest and I expect that I'll do some publicity around it. Some of this may involve television and radio appearances in both Ireland and Britain so I think for your mum's sake and our father's sake that you should be are aware that ...'

'Look, what are you telling me for? It's nothing to do with me. It's nothing to do with me. Don't ever call me again. Goodbye.'

In February of this year I tried again; I sent Foli a brief, polite message on Facebook asking how our father was doing. He has not, as yet, replied.

*

As part of the research for this book I visited the now derelict St Joseph's Baby Home and, afterwards, found myself on the Ormeau Road in south Belfast. I called into a shop to buy a bar of chocolate. The man behind the counter was about sixty years old.

'Can I just say, son, your English is perfect. Where are you from?' he asked.

'Beechmount, Falls Road,' I said.

'No, where are you really from?'

'Beechmount,' I said and walked out of the shop.

Acknowledgements

While many names in this book have been changed to protect the guilty, some people deserve a special mention.

Jimmy Poland and Seamus Masterson – despite being in my late thirties (more or less!) I still haven't decided which of you is my 'best friend'. This task has been made all the more difficult by the arrival of Andrea O'Neill who has not only been a special friend over the past ten rollercoaster years, but also wears her lip gloss better than either of you two ever could.

A big thank you to Anita Cochrane for her constant support and suggestions and for allowing me to have the odd draw of her Marlboro cigarette over a coffee.

A group of journalists I met in 1998 have remained sources of support, friendship and endless coffees. My eternal thanks to Aeneas Bonner, John Manley, Paul McKillion and Ciara McGrillen, Eddie McCann and Paul Tanney. Good to see that an abysmal ability to write shorthand has not held any of you back. Here's to creativity on application forms! Thanks also to Laura Graham who has shown a great ability to put herself in my shoes even though our backgrounds are very different.

Thanks to my very patient agent Matthew Hamilton, to all the staff at Blackstaff Press and to Kate Shepherd and Gráinne Killeen. The Creative Writer's Network provided crucial help through Damian Gorman, and Sheena Wilkinson wielded her red pen to good effect.

Some of the years post jail have been very difficult and a few people went to extraordinary lengths to add to the bad times but I fought back with all my strength. The help of Des Fagan of the NUJ, Steve Tweed of Amicus and some legal eagles who know who they are was invaluable. There are many others I could mention but I have to stop at some point. Thank you all.

And so to jail. I am often asked if I am bitter about it. I am not. I don't think any republican prisoner wanted to be in jail, but opposition to the British was the life we all chose and jail was part of the process. I met some impressive, thoughtful, resourceful men and I learned a lot about life. Writing the chapters on Castlereagh, remand and the H-blocks meant negotiating some tricky and sensitive terrain. I thank Pat Sheehan, Pádraic Wilson and Danny Morrison for various tips and insights. I have tried to give an honest account of how the experience was for me without too much machismo and without revealing specific secrets. To use such information to sell books, make sensational allegations and smear former comrades is, for this writer, a betrayal.

To the people of Beechmout, Iveagh and Mica Drive I offer my gratitude for your support in helping me lead a life less ordinary.